German-American Genealogical Research
Monograph Number 22

FROM BREMEN TO AMERICA IN 1850:

FOURTEEN RARE EMIGRANT SHIP LISTS

Clifford Neal Smith

CLEARFIELD

First printing, June 1987 √ʃ
Reprint, March 1988   qz
Reprint, October 1988   qz
Reprint, September 1989   qz
Reprint, November 1990   qz
Reprint, August 1993   u
Reprint, January 1995   u
Reprint, May 1996   u
Reprint, March 1997   u

Reprinted for
Clearfield Company, Inc. by
Genealogical Publishing Co., Inc.
Baltimore, Maryland
2004

International Standard Book Number: 0-8063-5226-4

Made in the United States of America

CONTENTS

*A return trip from New York to Bremen.

INTRODUCTION

There is little so rare in German-American genealogy as a complete emigrant passenger list from Bremen. During the second world war the massive records of emigration through the port of Bremen were burned; only here and there have transcripts survived. Hereinafter will be found fourteen such lists dating from 1850 which were published in an obscure weekly newspaper from Rudolstadt, Thuringia, entitled the Allgemeine Auswanderungs-Zeitung (General Emigration Newspaper), devoted to news about ship sailings, warnings about unscrupulous travel agents, and reports from immigrants in the New World.

The lists of emigrants are presented in alphabetical order. An attempt has been made to cross-reference individuals emigrating together (and who may relatives or close associates). Some ships carried large parties from the same village; entries for individuals in such parties usually include notations "with others", and researchers should check the entire ship list for their companions, because many of them may have settled near each other in the United States.

The Allgemeine Auswanderungs-Zeitung (AAZ) also published a number of lists from Hamburg (not reproduced in this monograph). Since the 1850 Hamburg lists have already been transcribed from the surviving police records preserved in the Hamburg archives,[1] this writer has compared the newspaper transcriptions with the original Hamburg police record, discovering that the names of cabin passengers were not included in the original records, presumably because the Hamburg police were only charged with the loading of steerage and between-deck emigrants. It is not known whether Bremen port officials followed a similar practice or whether ship captains included the names of cabin passengers in the lists they submitted to American officials at ports of entry. Consequently, cabin passengers are designated hereinafter with asterisks after their names as indication to researchers that these names may be missing from ship entry records in American ports of entry.

Exact citations have been included in each ship list heading as follows: Allgemeine Auswanderungs-Zeitung (AAZ), volume 4 (1850), page number. The newspaper will be found in the Beinecke Rare Book Collection of the Yale University Library.

1. Clifford Neal Smith, Reconstructed Passenger Lists for 1850: Hamburg to Australia, Brazil, Canada, Chile, and the United States. German and Central European Emigration, Monograph number 1, in four parts (McNeal, AZ: Westland Publications, 1980-1981).

List 1
Ship: <u>Itzstein und Welker</u> (Bremen flag)
Captain: Hinrich Bosse
Departure Date: 5 May 1850
From: Bremen
To: New Orleans
Passengers: First Class, 13 ; Steerage & Between-
   Deck, 251 persons (of which 9 babies)
Citation: AAZ (1850), 59:215

APEL, --, from Eisenach; with family of 5 & Mart.
   MEHLIG

BACKE, Theresia, from Luedinghausen

BAUER, Simon, from Krook

BAUMANN, J., from Emden

BAUMBACH, Georg, from Lichtenhagen

BECKE, Georg, from Zellerfeld

BECKER, Anna, from Elberfeld; with Hermann GOEBEL

BENSTEIN, Carl, from Nordkirchen; with wife

BERGHORN, Carl, from Schluesselburg; with Heinrich
   GRESE

BERGMANN, --, from Boetzow; with family of 9 & KRAUSE
   family of 5

BERK, --, from Bechlingen; with family of 8

BICKENBACK, Gottfr(ied), from Ruenderoth; with Franziska STEUR & Ann SCHAFFNER and their children

BLONN, H. Friederike, from Luetelsburg; with child

BOCLERT, Ludwig, from Hildesheim

BOEHS, Heinrich, from Sondershausen; with Justine

BOEHS, Justine, from Sondershausen; with Heinrich

BORGMANN, Joh(ann) Fr(iedrich), from Bramsche; with
   Marg(arethe) Elise

BORGMANN, Marg(arethe) Elise, from Bramsche; with
   Joh(ann) Fr(iedrich)

BORGMANN, Wilhelm, from Brockhorst

BRAUER, --,* from Goerlitz; with family of 8

BRENNECKE, Gust(av) Wilh(elm), from Duesseldorf

BUECKENER, Joseph, from Glandorf

BUEHNEMANN, Joh(ann) H., from Seeste

BURCHHARD, Mich(ael), from Houston

BUSSE, Friedrich, from Sage; with Carl Ludwig STRUNK
   & Friedrich REEDE

BUTKE? (or BUTTE?), Friedrich, from Sotte

DEGENHART, Cath(erine), from Pfaffschwende; with
   Dorothea

DEGENHART, Dorothea, from Pfaffschwende; with Cath-
   (erine)

DEPPE, Wilh(elm), from Gr(oss) Schnee

DRESCHER, Ferd(inand), from Jena; with Emilie ROPP

DRESSEL, Cath(arine) Barb(ara), from Brettendorf;
   with child

DREWES, --, from Brocklage; with family of 5

DUEHNLUKE, H., from Verrel

ENERBUSCH, Caroline, from Altena; with RUMP family

ENGEL, Emma*, from Bussadingen

ERKEL, Georg, from Wiesbaden

FEIERTAG, Val(entin), from Pfaffschwende; with others

FREUND, --, from Gelshausen

FROMM, Georg, of Pfaffschwende; with others

GIESELMEYER, Wilh(elm), from Oberbecksen; with others

GILLE, Joh(ann), from Pfaffschwende; with others

GOEBEL, Hermann, from Elberfeld; with Anna BECKER

GOEKE, Anton, from Beverungen; with Clemens

GOEKE, Clemens, from Beverungen; with Anton

GOPPELMANN, Heinrich, from Nienburg

GRAENICHER, Hans, from Zosingen

GRESE, Heinrich, from Schluesselburg; with Carl BERG-
   HORN

GRIESELMANN, --, from Oberbecksen; family of 3 & with
   many others

GROESCHNER, --, from Meura; with 3? (or 4?) siblings

GUTMANN, Anna, from Bodman

HAHNE, --, from Oberbecksen; with family of 7 & many
   others

HAHNE, Christ(ian), from Oberbecksen; with many others

HANHOFF, Joseph, from Nordwald; with Anton zum HASCH

HARBERT, Gustav, from Rotenburg; with wife

HARTKE, Joh(ann) H., from Esse

HASCH (or ZUM HASCH), Anton, from Nordwald; with Joseph HANHOFF

HASENJAEGER, --, from Oberbecksen; with family of 10
   & many others

HENTZMANN, --, from Hamburg; with wife

HILDEBRANDT, Albert, from Walle; with wife

HOFFMANN, Cath(erine), from Herzogenreuth; with child

1

HUEPER, --, from Varel

ILLESE, Fried(rich), from Hannover; with Heinrich RIEKE

ITERMEYER, --, from Rehme; with family of 10 & Friedrich KOERTNER

JEPE, Wilh(elmine) Gertrude, from Iburg

KAMPERT, Franz, from Suedkirchen

KIMMEL, Carl, from Lichtringen; with Friedrich KOERNER

KOERNER, Friedrich, from Lichtringen; with Carl KIMMEL

KOERTNER, Friedrich, from Rehme; with ITERMEYER family

KRAEMER, F., from Achmer; with Johann ROTHERT

KRAEMER, Fr(iedrich), from Blasheim; with Henriette SCHUETTE & Johann MEYER

KRAMER, Johann, from Forsthaus

KRAUSE, --, from Boetzow; with family of 5 & BERGMANN family of 9

KRAUSE, Adam, from Hombrechtshausen

KUBISCH, H., from Goerlitz; with J. MARTINY

LIEBMANN, Phil(ipp), from Altkrautheim

LINZ, Ernst, from Altenburg

LORENZ, Marg(arethe), from Tueckelhaus

LORIUS, Henry P., from La Heuthe

MACHELEDT, Fr(iedrich) Berth(old?), from Dienstedt

MARTINY, J., from Goerlitz; with H. KUBISCH

MEHLIG, Mart(in? or Martine?), from Eisenach; with APEL family

MEYER, Charlotte, from Halen; with H. Adolf VINKE

MEYER, Joh(ann), from Blasheim; with Friedrich KRAEMER & Henriette SCHUETTE

MEYER, Joh(ann) Fr(iedrich), from Germold

MONTAG, Joh(ann), from Pfaffschwende; with others

MUELLER, J. H., from Loeningen

NAEMMLAEPP, --, from Berum; with family of 6

NEUBAUER, Fr(iedrich) Ludw(ig), from Singen

NEUBERT, Theodor, from Langenwiese; with August SCHUHMANN

NOLTING, Louise, from Oberbecksen; with many others

OSTER, Paul, from Elsenz

PINGEL, Ant(on), from Plettenberg; with wife

PLAHT, C.*, from Berlin; with wife

PLUMHOFF, Ernst A., from Wellendorf

RASCH, Johann, from Holwiese

REEDE, Friedrich, from Sage; with Friedrich BUSSE & Carl Ludwig STRUNK

REHBEIN, Carl, from Lauenfoerde; with Mathilde

REHBEIN, Mathilde, from Lauenfoerde; with Carl

REICHERZER, C. V.*, from Rinteln, with wife

REINEBACH, C. F., from Hevern

RICKERTS, F. U., from Hage

RIEKE, Heinrich, from Hannover; with Friedrich ILLESE

ROPP, Emilie, from Jena; with Ferdinand DRESCHER

ROSCHE, --, from Warstein; with family of 10

ROSCHE, August, from Warstein; with Franz & -- ROSCHE (family of 10)

ROSCHE, Franz, from Warstein; with August & -- ROSCHE (family of 10)

ROSENKRANZ, --, from Behrwalde; with family of 7

ROTHERT, Joh(ann), from Achmer; with F. KRAEMER

RUECHEL, Clara, from Pfaffschwende; with V. & Gottfried; & many others

RUECHEL, Gottfr(ied), from Pfaffschwende; with V. & Clara; many others

RUECHEL, V., from Pfaffschwende; with Clara & Gottfried & many others

RUMP, --, from Altena; with family of 4 & Caroline ENERBUSCH

RUSSEL, Christ(ian), from Hohnhorst

SAARHAYE, Heinrich, from Hesseln

SARBERG, Herm(ann) Rud(olph), from Pente

SCHAFFNER, Anna, from Ruenderoth; with child, Gottfried BICKENBACK & Franziska STEUR (with child)

SCHEIDEMANN, Johann, from Lutterberg; with wife

SCHMIDT, --, from Coburg; with family of 3

SCHMITZ, Carl, from Wierst

SCHNEIDER, Joh(ann), from Vollenburg; with wife

SCHOPPE, Hermann, from Muenster

SCHROEDER, --, from Braunschweig; with family of 4

SCHUETTE, Henriette, from Blasheim; with Friedrich KRAEMER & Johann MEYER

SCHULMANN, August, from Langenwiese; with Theodor
    NEUBERT

STAMM, Amalie, from Himmelsthuer; with Elise

STAMM, Elise, from Himmelsthuer; with Amalie

STEMMLER, --, fro Kutzbrunn; with family of 4

STENDER, Carl, from Geismar

STEUR, Ranziska, from Ruenderoth; with child & Gott-
    fried BICKENBACK & Anna SCHAFFNER (& child)

STRUNK, Carl Ludwig, from Sage; with Friedrich BUSSE
    & Friedrich REEDE

STUMPFF, Rud(olph), from Schwerin

TRUTE, Heinrich, from Osterode

UHLE, Carl, from Oberbecksen; with wife & many others

USCHNER, Carl Rud(olph), Dr., from Loebau

VINKE, H. Adolf, from Halen; with Charlotte MEYER

WEISSERT, Christine, from Helmstadt; with Elisabeth

WEISSERT, Elisabeth, from Helmstadt; with Christine

WESSLING, Heinrich, from Burgsteinfurt; with wife

WIHNSMEYER, --, from Niederbecksen; with family of 5

WULF, Herm(ann), from Seeste

ZINKE, Chr(istian) Fr(iedrich), from Bischoffsroda

ZOELLNER, --, from Oberbecksen; with family of 4 &
    many others

ZUM HASCH, Anton, from Nordwald; with Joseph HANHOFF

List 2
Ship: George Washington
Captain: -- Probst
Departure Date: 7 May 1850
From: Bremen
To: San Francisco
Passengers: First Class, 14 persons; Between-Deck,
    16 persons
Citation: AAZ 4:66:264

BOESER, Bernh(ard)*, from Bremen; with others

BOESER, G. W.*, from Bremen; with others

BULTMANN, H.*, from Bremen; with others

BUSCHMANN, H., from Bremen; with others

DE HAAN, L. J., from Emden

DUISENBERG, Mad(eline?)*, from Bremen; with others

ECKERLAND, Carl, from Koenigsberg

FLACHSBART, H., from Bremen; with others

HAAN, L. J. de, from Emden

HAMMERS, Diedr(ich), from Bremen; with others

HELMKEN, Th.*, from Bremen; with others

HILLMANN, H., from Bramstadt

IDE, W(ilhel)m, from Bremen; with others

KATZ, Dan(iel), from Bremen; with others

KORFF, Diedr(ich), from Bremen; with Johann H.

KORFF, Johann H., from Bremen; with Diedrich

KRAUSS, W., from Kupferzell

LAKEMANN, W(ilhel)m*, from Hameln; with August & Wil-
    helm MARQUARDT

MARQUARDT, August*, from Hameln; with Wilhelm MAR-
    QUARDT & Wilhelm LAKEMANN

MARQUARDT, W(ilhel)m*, from Hameln; with August MAR-
    QUARDT & Wilhelm LAKEMANN

MENSING, Mad(eline?)*, from Bremen; with others

MUELLER, Jac(ob)*, from Bad Ems

OHLDEMEYER, Fr(iedrich), from Stolzenau

RIEKMERS, Pauline*, from Bremen; with others

RUEHLING, Ed(uard)*, from Hamburg

SCHMITZ, Nic(olaus), from Paderborn

SCHUBERT, G., from Schieritz

SPETHMANN, Carl, from Holstein

STAMM, Emil Victor*, from Bremen; with others

WEISSHAAR, Carl Andr(eas), from Hannover

WIDMER, Isaac, from St. Gallen

List 3
Ship: Helene (Bremen flag)
Captain: -- Bolkmann
Departure Date: 29 May 1850
From: Bremen
To: New York
Passengers: First Class, 18 persons; Steerage & Be-
    tween-Deck, 268 persons
Citation: AAZ 4:68:271

ABNER, Christ(ian) Mar(cus?), from Walbach

AI, Ad(olph) Jos(eph), from Huenfeld; with Wiena BON-
    ERT

ALFKEN, Anna, from Rottenfelde; with others

ARNOLDI, --, Miss*, place or origin not given

BAER, Herm(ann), from Colberg

BANDEL, Arn(hold?) von, from Hannover

BARLET, Hugo, from Bamberg

BARTELS, Chr(istian), from Leidhorst; with August
    FISCHER & Christian SCHOPPE

BEHRENS, Bernh(ard), from Volkmarsen

BERLING, Fr(an)z, from Berching; with family of 7

BOCK, Heinr(ich), from Friedewald; with family of 4
    & Anna Margarethe HERBER

BOCK, Heinr(ich), from Dallhausen; with Wilhelm MAN-
NEL

BOCK, Heinrich, from Hilmes

BOETJER, --, Miss, from Osterholz

BOHRAN, Cath(arine) Carol(ine), from Gr(oss) Dohren-
    berg; with Friedrich Wi8helm WOEHRMANN

BONERT, Wiena, from Huenfeld; with Adolph Joseph AI

BORCHELT, Aug(ust), from Rehren; with Friedrich
    GOERTZ

BREDEHORST, Anna, from Bremen; with Margarethe

BREDEHORST, Marg(arethe), from Bremen; with Anna

BREHL, Andr(eas), from Langenbieber

BREUER, Louis, from Marklessa; with family of 3

BROMM, Charlotte, from Emden; with family of 3

BRUEGGEMANN, Carl, from Wagenfeld

BRUENJES, H., from Rottenfelde; with others

BRUMLOP, Marie*, from Bremen; with others

BUCHERER, Jul(ius?), from Neunhardt

BUSCHKAEMPER, Gerh(ard), from Diestedde

COHN, Mich(ael), from Ritterhude

CORDES, H., from Uterlande

CRAMER, Ph(ilipp?), from Volkmarsen; with Heinrich
    GOTHMANN

DAEUBLE, --, Miss*, from Stuttgart

DEHN, Anna, from Westerbeck; with Magnus Christian
    FINKE

DEICHMANN, Johann, from Gr(oss) Almerode; with G.
    SEITZ

DENGLER, Joh(ann), from Berching; with family of 2

DEUTLINGER, Jac(ob), from Seedorf

DOEBELING, Gottl(ieb?), from Muenden; with Louis
    KROELING

DUERKOP, Carol(ine) from Seiboldshausen; with Minna

DUERKOP, Minna, from Seiboldshausen; with Caroline

EBELING, Carol(ine), from Leese; with Conrad EBELING,
    Wilhelm HILMANN, & August ILSE

EBELING, Conr(ad), from Leese; with Caroline EBELING,
    Wilhelm HILMANN, & August ILSE

ECKSTEIN, Anna, from Binsberg; with G. EISMANN &
    Catharine STAEHR

EISMANN, G., from Binsberg; with Anna ECKSTEIN &
    Catharine STAEHR

ENNEN, P. F. A., from Schwein

FICKEN, Anna, from Bremen; with Haase family

FINKE, Magnus Chr(istian), from Westerbeck; with
    Anna DEHN

FISCHER, August, from Leidhorst; with Christian BAR-
    TELS & Christian SCHOPPE

FISCHER, Beta, from Uterlande

FISCHER, G., from Ransbach

FISCHER, Joh(ann), from Rottenfelde; with others

FLOETHMANN, Oscar, from Buttstedt; with August KLUGE,
    Carl HAHN, & Carl F. URBAN

FRIEDRICH, Otto, from Appenrod; with family of 3

FRIELING, H., from Rottenfelde; with others

FURTMUELLER, Jac(ob), from Stammheim; with Gottlieb
    SCHUMACHER

GADESMANN, Henriette, from Eldagsen

GOELLNER, Renke, from Strickhausen

GOERTZ, Fr(iedrich), from Rehren; with family of 4

GOLDSCHMIDT, Val(entin), from Hofbieber

GOTHMANN, H(ei)nr(ich), from Volkmarsen; with Philipp
    CRAMER

GROTE, Heinr(ich), from Winzlar; with family of 2 &
    H. KIELMEYER, & Friedrich HOMEYER

GUETTICH, Ludwig, from Landsbergen

GUTTENBERGER, Marg(arethe), from Berching; with others

HAASE, Auguste, from Bremen; with Mathilde, Louise, &
    Mrs. -- HAASE, & Anna FICKEN

HAASE, Louise, from Bremen; with Auguste, Mathilde, &
    Mrs. -- HAASE, & Anna FICKEN

HAASE, Mathilde, from Bremen; with Auguste, Louise, &
    Mrs. -- HAASE, & Anna FICKEN

HAASE, --, Mrs., from Bremen; with Auguste, Louise, Mathilde HAASE, & Anna FICKEN

HAHN, Carl, from Buttstedt; with August KLUGE, Oscar FLOETHMANN, & Carl F. URBAN

HALENBECK, Ludwig, from Rottenfelde; with others

HALLENBERGER, Ferd(inand), from Rennert(s)chhausen

HARTJE, H(ein)r(ich?), from Hallstedt; with Wilhelm

HARTJE, W(ilhel)m, from Hallstedt; with Heinrich

HAUFF? (or HAUSS?), Theod(or), from Waldbusch

HEBBELER, Chr(istian) H., from Schledehausen; with Anna F. NIEMANN

HEINZE, Fr(iedrich), from Bottendorf; with family of 10 & Johann SIELING

HENNINGS, --, from Verden? (Berden?)

HERBER, Anna Mar(garethe), from Friedewald; with Heinrich BOCK

HERBER, Heinr(ich), from Kleinroda

HILMANN? (HILMAUNN?), W(ilhel)m, from Leese; with August ILSE, Caroline & Conrad EBELING

HOLTZMANN (or HOLZMANN), Joh(ann), from Kauernhofen; with family of 9

HOLZNER, Joh(ann), from Wuerzburg

HOMEYER, Fr(iedrich), from Winzlar; with family of 8, & H. KIELMEYER, & H. GROTE

HOPPE, Gottfr(ied), from Hamm; with family of 4

ILSE, Aug(ust), from Leese; with Wilhelm HILMANN, Caroline & Conrad EBELING

ISENSEE, Heinr(ich), from Rottenfelde; with others

JAEGER, Joh(ann), from Hilmes

JONAS, G., from Redershausen

JUDIESCH, Fr(iedrich), from Schmarsow; with family of 5 & Carl VOELKER

KAEUFLER, Marg(arethe) El(isabeth), from Niederurf; with Anna C. & Philipp KLIPP, Conrad WEISS

KAPPIS, Gustav, from Tuebingen

KEULING, Carl, from Basbeck

KIELMEYER, Heinrich, from Winzlar; with family of 4 & Heinrich GROTE & Friedrich HOMEYER

KLINGE, Fr(iedrich), from Einbeck

KLIPP, Anna Cath(arine), from Niederurf; with Anna C. & Philipp KLIPP, Conrad WEISS, & Margarethe Elisabeth KAEUFLER

KLIPP, Ph(ilipp?), from Niederurf; with Anna C. KLIPP, Conrad WEISS & Margarethe Elisabeth KAEUFLER

KLOTZBACH, Joh(ann), from Mansfeld; with Valentin

KLOTZBACH, Ther(esia?), from Grossenbach

KLOTZBACH, Val(entin) from Hilmes; with Johann

KLUGE, Aug(ust), from Buttstedt; with Carl HAHN, Oscar FLOETHMANN, & Carl Friedrich URBAN

KROELING, Louis, from Muenden; with family of 2 & Gottlieb DOEBELING

KROPP, H. L.*, from Varel

KRUHOEFFER, Fr(iedrich), from Gellershausen

LEMMER, Joh(ann), from Sichertshausen

LEONHARDI, W(ilhel)m, from Mengerin; with Eduard STIEFEL

LINDEMANN, Carl, from Grambke; with family of 3

LOEWE, Fr(iedrich), from Asbach

LUEHRS, Claus, from Lorstedt; with A. BOEHLKEN

LUESSEN, Hur., from Scharmbeck; with Diedrich OETERS

MACKEROTH, Heinrich, from Reusees; with family of 5 & Margarethe STRECKER

MALEK, Jac(ob), from Meiningen; with Barbara SCHORR & Ludwig ZOELLNER

MANNEL, W(ilhel)m, from Dallhausen; with Heinrich BOCK

MARST, Cath(arine), from Altbuhlach; with Johann

MARST, Joh(ann), from Altbuhlach; with Catharine

MEHRTENS, G., from Lorstedt? (Loxstedt?)

MENGERT, Beta*, from Bremen; with Pastor J. H. MENGERT, & others

MENGERT, J. H., pastor, from Bremen; with Beta MENGERT & others

MOGK, Casp(ar), from Grebenau; with family of 3

MURTFELD, Louis*, from Bremen; with others

NACHTIGALL, Hel(ene?), from Hildesheim

NIEMANN, Anna Fr(iedrike?), from Schledehausen; with Christian H. HEBBELER

NOLTENIUS, J. D.*, from Bremen; with others

OETERS, Diedr(ich), from Scharmbeck; with Hur. LUESSEN

PETERS, Eilert, from Colmar; with family of 7

PFAHLER, Willibald, from Berching; with family of 4

PFEIFFER, Fr(iedrich), from Alzenberg

PLOEGER, Dor(othea?), from Polle

RALL, --, Miss*, from Basel

RATHJEN, Mad(eline?)*, place of origin not given; with 4 children

REGENTHAL, W(ilhel)m, from Batzhausen

REHBEIN, A., from Asbach; with Elisabeth

REHBEIN, El(isabeth?), from Asbach; with A. REHBEIN

REICH, Joh(ann), from Kuehndorf

REINFELDER, Emma, from Nuernberg; with Jul(iane? or Julius?)

REINFELDER, Jul(iane? or Julius?), from Nuenberg; with Emma

REISING, W(ilhel)m, from Diepholz

RESING, Joh(ann), from Gieselberg

RIES, H., from Hilmes

ROEH, --, from Dortrecht

ROEHLKEN, Alb., from Lorstedt

ROTTENFELD, Dina, from Rottenfelde; with F. ROTTEN-FELD

ROTTENFELD, F., from Rottenfelde; with Dina

SAFFER, G., from Kauernhofen; with family of 2 & Joseph SAFFER

SAFFER, Jos(eph), from Kauernhofen; with G. SAFFER

SCHLEGEMILCH, J. S., from Ragelstedt; with H. C. WEISSENBORN

SCHMIDT, Elise*, from Klagenfurt

SCHOPPE, Chr(istian), from Leidhorst

SCHORR, Barb(ara), from Meiningen; with Jacob MALEK & Ludwig ZOELLNER

SCHRIEVER, Jan., from Utherslande

SCHUETZ, Carl, from Herrnhausen

SCHUMACHER, Gottl(ieb?), from Stammheim; with Jacob FURTMUELLER

SEITZ, G., from Gr(oss) Almerode; with Johann DEICH-MANN

SENTEN, -- Van, from Emden

SIELING, Joh(ann), from Bottendorf; with Friedrich HEINZE

SILBER, Meyer, from Hildesheim

SPRINGMEYER, W(ilhel)m, from Rottenfelde; with others

STAEHR, Cath(arine), from Binsberg; with G. EISMANN & Ann ECKSTEIN

STELLJES, Joh(ann), from Ahrensfeld; with Diedrich WENDELKEN

STIEFEL, Ed(uard), from Mengeringhausen; with Wilhelm LEONHARDI

STRACKE, Alb., from Wildungen; with Louise

STRACKE, Louise, from Wildungen; with Alb.

STRECKER, Joh(ann), from Reusees; with Margarethe STRECKER & Heinrich MACKEROTH

STRECKER, Marg(arethe), from Reusees; with Jacob STRECKER & Heinrich MACKEROTH

STUEBNER, --, from Gera; with family of 8 & Johann VOELKEL

TAUSCHER, Henr(ich), from Glauchau; with family of 3

THIELE, Melch(ior?), from Christal; with family of 3

TIETJEN, A., from Rottenfelde; with others

URBAN, Carl Fr(iedrich), from Buttstedt; with August KLUGE, Carl HAHN, & Oscar FLOETHMANN

VAN SENTEN, --, from Emden

VEIT, C. H.*, from Schweinfurt

VOELKEL, Joh(ann), from Gera; with -- STUEBNER

VOELKER, Carl, from Schmarsow; with Friedrich JUDIESCH

VOIGTLAENDER, Dor(othea?) El(isabeth?), from Lindstedt

VON BANDEL, Arn(hold?)*, from Hannover

WALTER, Chr(istian), from Portenhagen

WEINBERG, Ros(ine?), from Scharmbeck

WEISS, Conr(ad), from Niederurf; with Anna C. & Philipp KLIPP & Margarethe Elisabeth KAEUFLER

WEISSBROD, Ludw(ig), from Wolfshausen

WEISSENBORN, H. C., from Ragelstedt; with J. S. SCHLEGEMILCH

WENDELKEN, Diedr(ich), from Ahrensfeld; with Johann STELLJES

WERNER, Fr(iedrich), from Wehrda

WETJEN, Gesert, from New York; with family of 4

WILCKENS, Heinr(ich), from Achim

WILHELM, A. C.*, from Oldenburg

WOEHRMANN, Fr(iedrich) W(ilhel)m, from Gr(oss) Dohrenberg; with Catharine C. BOHRAN

WOHLEN, Alb., from Neubruechhausen

WREDEN, Mart(in), from Neuenfeld

WUEHRMANN, Joh(ann), from Bensen (or Beusen)

WULF, Herm(ann), from Rottenfelde; with others

ZOELLNER, Ludwig, from Meiningen; with Jacob MALEK & Barbara SCHORR

List 4
Ship: <u>America</u>
Captain: -- Gaetjen
Departure Date: 10 Jun 1850
From: Bremen
To: New York
Passengers: First Class, 11 persons; Steerage & Be-
    tween-Deck, 170 persons
Citation: AAZ, 4:71:283

ALBUS, W(ilhel)m, from Huettingen

ALFKEN, Marg(arethe), from Besse; with family of 3 &
    H. MEYER

ALLGEIER, Cath(arine), from Deiningen

AMMON, F. A., from Neukirchen

AUSTERMANN, B. W., from Everswinkel; with Theodor
    AUSTERMANN & Bernhard KORTEJOHANN

AUSTERMANN, Th(eodor? or Thomas?), from Everswinkel;
    with B. W. AUSTERMANN & Bernhard KORTEJOHANN

BEIER, Magd(alene), from Hettenhausen; with Mathias

BEIER, Mathias, from Hettenhausen; with Magdalene

BENNING, W., from Kleinern; with Christian KOHL &
    Carl VOGEL

BIERMANN, C., from Sattenhausen

BOCK, Conr(ad), from Hilpoldstein

BOEHME, J. G., from Dresden; with Friedrich FISCHER &
    C. F. BREIER

BREIER, C. F., from Dresden; with J. G. BOEHME &
    Friedrich FISCHER

BRUCHER, Am.*, from Koenigsberg; with others

BRUESS, W(ilhel)m, from Eichsier

CARLEY, Albertine, from Halberstadt

CORSEPIUS, Otto, from Koenigsberg; with others

DAHME, Lina, from Muenster; with Caroline NIEHOF &
    Hermann OENECK

EBERT, Alex(ander), from Koenigsberg; with others

EBERT, F., from Rotholz

ELSAESSER, Joh(ann), from Volmerz; with family of 7 &
    Sabine SCHREIBER

ERDMANN, Rob(ert), from Borken; with Dina ROSENBUSCH

FISCHER, Fr(iedrich), from Dresden; with J. G. BOEHME
    & C. F. BREIER

FLAMMER, W(ilhel)m, from Jebenhausen; with family of
    3

FLEISCHMANN, G. A., from Koenigsberg; with others

FLEISCHMANN, Joh(ann), from Weidenau; with Joseph
    KERL, Barbara MEYER, & Alois MEYZEN

FORSBERG, A. O., from Koenigsberg; with family of 3 &
    others

FORSBERG, C. W.*, from Koenigsberg; with others

FRAENKEL, Jette, from Diespeck; with Sarah FRAENKEL,
    Babette HOLZBERGER, & Babette GENER

FRAENKEL, Sarah, from Diespeck; with Jette FRAENKEL,
    Babette HOLZBERGER, & Babette GENER

FREESE, R. A., from Koenigsberg; with others

FUCHS, --, Mrs., from Koenigsberg; with family of 3 &
    others

GENER, Bab(ette?), from Diespeck; with Jette & Sarah
    FRAENKEL, & Babette HOLZBERGER

GLATZ, H. A.*, from Koenigsberg; with others

GOETZ, Ferd(inand), from Laub

GRAETZ, Fr(iedrich), from Berlin

GUSMANN, Aug(ust), from Koenigsberg; with others

HARTMANN, C., from Hemford; with family of 4

HAU, Anna Marg(arethe), from Ulmbach; with Nicolaus

HAU, Nic(olaus), from Ulmbach; with Anna Margarethe

HAUSMANN, Ed(uard), from Eschendorf; with family of 2

HEIDTMANN, C., from Wernignhausen; with H. C. KAUFMANN

HERMANN, W., from Koenigsberg; with others

HERZ, Jette, from Furth; with Fanni POTSCHER

HILLENBRANDT, Jos(eph), from Boehmentich; with Anton
    SCHMIDT

HOEPKEN, --, Miss*, from Koenigsberg; with others

HOFFER, Rebecca, from Cassel

HOLSTEIN, A., from Muenster

HOLZBERGER, Bab(ette?), from Diespeck; with Jette &
    Sarah FRAENKEL, & Babette GENER

JOHN, Fr(iedrich)*, from Koenigsberg; with others

JOSTY, G., from Davas; with family of 3

KASSEBER, A., from Gronau

KAUFMANN, H. C., from Werninghausen; with C. HEIDTMANN

KERL, Jos(eph), from Weidenau; with Johann FLEISCHMANN,
    Babara MEYER, & Alois MEYZEN

KEUSS, Ad(olph), from Kegelsdorf; with family of 3

KILIAN, Chr(istian), from Ummerstadt

KITZSTEINER, Joh(ann), from Altmannsdorf; with family
    of 3

KLEINE, --, from Wildeshausen

KOHL, Chr(istian), from Kleinern; with W. BENNING & Carl VOGEL

KORTEJOHANN, Bernh(ard), from Everswinkel; with B. W. & Th. AUSTERMANN

KUEBLER, J., from Goeppingen

KURZE, W(ilhel)m, from Treppershausen; with H. MICHEL

KUTZKY, C. A., from Schloppe; with A. SCHULTZ

LANGE, Joh(ann), from Besse

LEPPERT, Barb(ara), from Lembach

MAGD, Anna Mar(garethe? or Maria?), from Oberdingen-heim; with family of 2

MARDORF, Bernh(ard), from Utenborn; with Minna MURHARD, & Wilhelmine OTTO

MEYER, Barb(ara), from Weidenau; with Johann FLEISCH-MANN, Joseph KERL, & Alois MEYZEN

MEYER, H., from Besse; with Margarethe ALFKEN

MEYER, Joh(ann), from Waltersberg; with family of 5

MEYZEN, Alois, from Weidenau; with Johann FLEISCHMANN, Joseph KER*, & Barbara MEYER

MICHEL, H., from Treppershausen; with Wilhelm KURZE

MOELLER, Chr(istian), from New York

MOELLERS, W(ilhel)m, from Brochterbeck; with family of 2

MUENCH, H., from Gellershausen

MURHARD, Minna, from Utenborn; with Bernhard MARDORF, Wilhelmine OTTO

MUTSCHLER, Jos(eph), from Hechingen

NIEHOF, Carol(ine), from Muenster; with Lina DAHME & Hermann OENECK

NITSCHE, Sophie, from Nitschka

NOLL, H., from Hofkalbsburg

NOMMINGER? (ROMMINGER?), Andr(eas), from Tuttlingen

OENECK, Herm(ann), from Muenster; with Lina DAHME & Caroline NIEHOF

OTTO, Conrad, from Utenborn; with Wilhelmine OTTO, Bernhard MARDORF, & Minna MURHARD

OTTO, Wilhelmine, from Utenborn; with Conrad OTTO, Bernhard MARDORF, & Minna MURHARD

PAUSSF, Jul(ius?, Juliane?), from Neussis? (Reussis?); with Const. SCHUCHARDT

POTSCHER, Fanni, from Furth; with Jette HERZ

PRELLER, Wilhelm(ine?), from Upferstedt

REBHAHN, J. G., from Coburg; with J. P. RENNER

RECKUM, Ad(olph), from Essen

REICHARD, Gottl(ieb?), from Carbussen

REIS, Anna Cath(arine), from Rhuenda; with Just. REIS, August, H., & Trinch. RIEDER

REIS, Just(ine?), from Rhuenda; with Anna Catharine REIS & August, H., & Trinch. RIEDER

REISSENWEBER, Nic(olaus), from Wuerlsdorf; with family of 6

RENNER, J. P., from Coburg; with J. G. REBHAHN

REULEIN, Barb(ara), from Lehmingen; with Johann REU-LEIN & H. VOLK

REULEIN, Joh(ann), from Lehmingen; with Barbara REU-LEIN & H. VOLK

REUTER, Hubert, from Hochheim; with family of 6

RIEDER, Aug(ust), from Rhuenda; with H. & Trinch.

RIEDER, H., from Rhuenda; with August & Trinch. & Anna & Just. REIS

RIEDER, Trinch., from Rhuenda; with August & H. RIEDER & Anna & Just. REIS

ROMMINGER? (NOMMINGER?), Andr(eas), from Tuttlingen

ROSENBUSCH, Dina, from Borken; with Robert ERDMANN

ROSENTHAL, W., from Koenigsberg; with others

SCHMEDES, F. H., from Breuna

SCHMIDT, Ant(on), from Boehmentich; with family of 2 & Joseph HILLENBRANDT

SCHREIBER, Sab(ine?), from Volmerz; with Johann EL-SAESSER & family

SCHUCHARDT, Const., from Neussis? (Reussis?); with Jul. PAUSSE

SCHULTZ, A., from Schloppe; with C. A. KUTZKY

SCHWAGER, Mich(ael), from Lochenbach

SOMMER, Xaver, from Lauternhofen

SPIELBUSCH, H., from Moehler

STEIN, Pet(er), from Linge8bach; with family of 2

STEINHAEUSER, A., from Leibingen

STEINWEG, Minna, from Bodendeich

STEPKE, Fr(iedrich), from Koenigsberg; with others

STREBEL, Dor(othea?), from Kuelsheim; with Leonhard

STREBEL, Leonh(ard), from Kuelsheim; with Dorothea

TEWES, Fr(iedrich), from Wildungen; with family of 2

VOGEL, Carl, from Kleinern; with Christian KOHL & W. BENNING

VOLK, H., from Lehmingen; with Barbara & Johann REULEIN

WIRTH, Rob(ert), place of origin not given

WITT, Ad(olph), from Koenigsberg; with others

WOLFF, C., from Niederrossla

ZIEGELMILLER, Jos(eph), from Dinkelsbuehl; with family of 5

ZIEGLER, Joh(ann), from Bischofsheim; with family of 2

List 5
Ship: Ocean
Captain: -- Jansen
Departure Date: 6 Jun 1850
From: Bremen
To: Baltimore
Passengers: First Class, 7 persons; Steerage & Between-Decks, 226 persons
Citation: AAZ, 4:71:283-284

ALTHOFF, Joh(ann), from Gleiner

AMMER, Joh(ann), from Reutlingen; with family of 3 & J. KRETZINGER, A. FOCHTMANN, & F. KNAPP

ANKELL, Heinr(ich), from Reutlingen; with others

BAER, H., from Wehlitz

BANGERT, Ludw(ig), from Mengeringhausen

BAUER, August, from Nuernberg; with L. M. BAUER

BAUER, L. M., from Adelshofen; with family of 2 & August BAUER

BAUMANN, Mar(cus? or Martin?), from Gelnhausen; with Friedrich LENZ & David HELLER

BAUMBACH, H., from Hoetzelrode; with family of 6

BAUMGARTEN, J., from Bauerbach

BEISSNER, Barb(ara), from Redlin

BEKLER, J. U., from Linden

BOEK, Gottl(ieb), from Reutlingen; with Jacob STECHENFINGER & Barbara HESS

BORN, W., from Zschecherchen; with Gustav & Karl HOFFMANN

BRANDENBURG, F. W., from Greifenhagen

BRAUER, J., from Armsfeld; with Tobias

BRAUER, Tob(ias?), from Armsfeld; with J. BRAUER

BRAUNS, --, from Stadtoldendorf

BREHM, Ant(on), from Schillingsfuerst

BRINGMANN, Joh(ann), from Bilshausen

BUEHLER, Fr(iedrich), from Reutlingen; with others

CHRIST, Chr(istian), from Elpenrod; with Marcus CHRIST & others

CHRIST, Mar(cus? or Martin?), from Elpenrod; with Christian CHRIST & others

CONRAD, Joh(ann) J., from Rainrod; with Margarethe GOTTRALD

DALLWIG, Mar(cus? or Martin), from Sinnersrode

DIETZ, Lor(enz?), from Braunau

DOTH, H. B. F., from Vechta; with Agnes HEYER & Anton FREYE

FAHLBUSCH, M. M., from Bassum

FESSLER, Mar(cus? or Martin?), from Heilbronn

FISCHER, Getr. (Gertrude?), from Cassel; with Elise SCHARRER

FOCHTMANN, Andr(eas), from Reutlingen; with J. AMMER, J. KRETZINGER, & F. KNAPP

FREIENSEENER, Elise, from Elpenrod; with others

FREWER, Ant(on), from Manrode

FREYE, Anton, from Vechta; with Agnes HEYER & H. B. F. DOTH

FUCHS, Leonh(ard), from Reubach; with J. A. REINHARD

GELHAUS, Aug(ust), from Manrode

GOETZ, Joh(ann) G., from Culmbach; with Barbara & Catharine MUENCH

GOLDBERG, Bend., from Oestinghausen

GOTTRALD, Marg(arethe), from Rainrod; with Johann J. CONRAD

GRAEF, Conr(ad), from Hutschdorf

GRAF, Anna, from Lutzendorf; with Margarethe GRAF & Georg HOHN

GRAF, Marg(arethe), from Lutzendorf; with Anna GRAF & Georg HOHN

GRIMMER, Dor(othea), from Ewaldsburg; with family of 2

HAHN, Aug(ust), from Selsingen

HAMEL, Elis(abeth), from Elpenrod; with family of 3 & others

HEIN, Egbert, from Hetzeldorf; with Johann ZEISSLER & Johann RICHTER

HEINBUCH, Fr(iedrich), from Schluechtern

HEINFELD, Joh(ann), from Flatterlon

HEINLEIN, A. M., from Ursprung; with Johann MEISTER

HELD, Mad(eline?)*, from Reutlingen

HELLER, Dav(id), from Gelnhausen; with Marcus BAUMANN & Friedrich LENZ

HESS, Barb(ara), from Reutlingen; with Jacob STECHEN-FINGER & Gottlieb BOEK

HEYDORN, Mar(cus? or Martin?), from Minden; with family of 4

HEYER, Agnes, from Vechta; with family of 2 & H. B. F. DOTH & Anton FREYE

HINZLER, Mar(cus? or Martin?), from Reitwangen

HIRSCHBERGER, Herm(ann), from Wichtringhausen

HOCHHEIM, E. W., from Werdorf; with Ernst KLEPPEL

HOEFER, Heinr(ich), from Hamme

HOFFMANN, Gust(av), from Zschecherchen; with Karl HOFFMANN & W. BORN

HOFFMANN, Karl, from Zschecherchen; with Gustav HOFF-MANN & W. BORN

HOHN, Georg, from Lutzendorf; with Anna & Margarethe GRAF

HOLLWEDE, Chr(istian), from Levern; with Th. MARWEDEL

HUEBSCH, M. R., from Dorfguetingen

HUMMEL, Jos(eph), from Reutlingen; with others

INSLER, Chr(istian), from Reutlingen; with others

JUST, Hedwig*, from Marburg

JUSTI, Heinr(ich), from Marburg

KACK, W., from Berghausen; with family of 5 & Gottfried MUELLER

KAMMER, J., from Rainrod; with family of 4

KAMPMANN, Heinr(ich), from Bavaria

KENNTER, Magd(alene?), from Hausen; with family of 6

KIPPLER, Dor(othea), from Pfullingen; with W. POEPLO, Marcus KLINGENSTEIN

KIRCHHEFER? (KIRCHHESER?), A. H., from Detern? (Oetern)

KLEPPEL, Ernst, from Werdorf; with family of 5 & E. W. HOCHHEIM

KLINGENSTEIN, Mar(cus? or Martin), from Pfullingen; with W. POEPLO & Dorothea KIPPLER

KLOESS, Ph(ilipp), from Bischoffthurn

KNAPP, Fr(iedrich), from Reutlingen; with J. AMMER, J. KRETZINGER, & A. FOCHTMANN

KOATNER, H., from Hundsdorf

KOEHLER, C. F., seifersdorf

KOEHNEN, Nanni, from Schweidnitz; with family of 3

KRAUSS, Elisab(eth), from Spulberg

KRETZINGER, Jac(ob), from Reutlingen; with J. AMMER, A. FOCHTMANN, & F. KNAPP

KRONER, Mart(in?), from Homenhausen; with Margarethe KRUMM

KRUEGER, Mar(cus? or Martin?), from Mennighoeffen; with family of 2

KRUMM, Marg(arethe), from Homenhausen; with Martin KRONER

LEBERMANN, Bernh(ard), from Ziegenhagen; with family of 2

LENZ, Fr(iedrich), from Gelnhausen; with Marcus BAU-MANN & David HELLER

LOEHEER, Heinr(ich), from Einbeck; with family of 3

LUEDEKE, J. R., from Nordhausen

MAROWSKY, L. W., from Berlin; with family of 3

MARWEDEL, Th(eodor? or Thomas?), from Levern; with Christian HOLLWEDE

MEISTER, Barb(ara), from Ursprung

MEISTER, Joh(ann), from Ursprung; with A. M. HEINLEIN

MENDEL, Jette, from Ovelgoenne

METTE, Joh(ann), from Solothurn; with family of 3

METZGER, Joh(ann), from Wanweil

MOGK, Jac(ob), from Weege

MOMBERGER, Joh(ann), from Elpenrod; with others

MUELLER, Gottfr(ied), from Berghausen; with family of 5 & W. KACK

MUELLER, H., from Epstadt

MUENCH, Barb(ara), from Culmbach; with Catharine MUENCH & Johann G. GOETZ

MUENCH, Cath(arine), from Culmbach; with Barbara MUENCH & Johann G. GOETZ

MUENDER, Gottl(ieb), from Reutlingen; with Jacob MUENDER & others

MUENDER, Jac(ob), from Reutlingen; with Gottlieb MUENDER & others

MULLER, H., from Hamburg

NEU? (REU?), G. M., from Sellgenstadt? (Selkenstadt?)

NICOLAUS, Joh(ann), from Elpenrod; with family of 4 & others

NIEMANN, Amalie, from Linden; with Betti

NIEMANN, Betti, from Linden; with Amalie

PALGEMEYER, Doris*, from Hamburg

PETZ, Joh(ann), from Reut8ingen; with others

POEPLO, W., from Pfullingen; with Dorothea KIPPLER &
Marcus KLINGENSTEIN

POLSTER, H., from Hundshaupt

REICH, Fr(iedrich), from Esslingen

REINHARD, J. A., from Reubach; with Leonhard FUCHS

REU? (NEU?), G. M., from Sellgenstadt? (Selkenstadt?)

RICHTER, Joh(ann), from Hetzeldorf; with Egbert HEIN
& Johann ZEISSLER

RITHMUELLER, Georg, from Asbach; with Andreas SCHMIDT

ROSENBERG, Marc(us?), from Niedermeisen

ROSENFELD, Isaac, from Buehne

RUEGELIN, Cath(arine), from Tuenfeld

SCHAEFER, Cath(arine), from Elpenrod; with others

SCHAEFER, Herm(ann), from Siegen; with family of 2

SCHARRER, Elise, from Cassel; with Getr. FISCHER

SCHAUMBURG, Jac(ob), from Odershausen; with Elisabeth
SYRING & Friedrich ULRICH

SCHLOSSER, H., from Elpenrod; with others

SCHMELZER, Fr(iedrich), from Rothenburg

SCHMIDT, Andr(eas), from Asbach; with Georg RITHMUEL-
LER

SCHMIDT, W., from Halle

SCHNEER, Ant(on), from Greven; with family of 9 &
B. H. STAPPELKAMPER

SCHOBER, Ferd(inand), from Coburg

SCHROEDER, Chr(istian) Ludw(ig), from Stammen; with
family of 3

SCHUKHARDT, Bitta*, from Ruettengen

SEEGER, Jac(ob)*, from Baltimore; with family of 3

SONNENLEITER, Mich(ael), from Wallhausen; with family
of 2

SPREEN, C. W., from Levern

STAPPELKAMPER, B. H., from Greven; with family of 2 &
Anton SCHNEER & family

STECHENFINGER, Jac(ob), from Reutlingen; with Barbara
HESS & Gottlieb BOEK

STERN, B. L., from Lipperade; with family of 10

STIEKAM, --, Mrs., from Pr(eussich?) Oldendorf; with
family of 4

SYRING, Elisab(eth), from Odershausen; with Jacob
SCHAUMBURG & Friedrich ULRICH

THIELEMANN, Pet(er), from Hueddingen

ULRICH, Fr(iedrich), from Odershausen; with Jacob
SCHAUMBURG & Elisabeth SYRING

WAGNER, Ad(olph), from Braunau

WAGNER, Louis, from Hameln

WEINBERG, Meier, from Burgsteinfurt

WELTNER, Adam, from Heimershausen; with Jacob & Anna
Margarethe

WELTNER, Anna Marg(arethe), from Heimershausen; with
Adam & Jacob

WELTNER, Jacob, from Heimershausen; with Adam & Anna
Margarethe

WENZEL, Gottfr(ied), from Neustadt

WESSLING, A., from Gehrde

WIDMANN, Fr(iedrich), from Stuttgart

ZEISSLER, Joh(ann), from Hetzeldorf; with Egbert HEIN
& Johann RICHTER

List 6
Ship: Orion
Captain: -- Schwartje
Departure Date: 22 Jun 1850
From: Bremen
To: New York
Passengers: First Class, 1; Steerage & Between-Deck,
139
Citation: AAZ 4:79:315

ARTZ, Gottfr(ied), from Salbecke; with family of 3

AUER, Joh(ann), from Lauten; with Magdalene & Margarethe SCHATTING

BAMANN, Rud(olph), from Berlin; with family of 4, Rudolph SCHMIDT & Charles RINOW

BARMANN? (BAXMANN?), Carl, from Bettmar; with family
of 3

BAXMANN, Carl. See Carl BARMANN

BOHN, Jac(ob), from Tambach; with family of 6 & Christian LEMMRICH

BORNEMANN, Heinr(ich), from Lippoldsberg

BOTHMER, H., from Niederscheden

BRUECK, Ludw(ig), from Giessen

BUCK, Dor(othea), from Hannover; with Johann & Henrich
HUGO

BUECHNER, Jac(ob), from Oberfuellbach; with family of 6 & Anna KESSEL & Georg ROSENBAUER

BURKHARD, Carol(ine), from Teichensfeld; with Theresia ELSASSER & Jacob FRAENKEL

BUSCHINGER, Cath(arine), from Streetau

DAUBERT, Herm(ann), from Altenburg; with J. SCHUMANN, L. WIETE, H. T. MUELLER, & A. THEILIG

DIETZ, B. C., from Koerner; with family of 3 & Erasmus WALTHER

DIPPEL, G., from Heidelbach; with family of 6

DRESSEL, H., from Hellingen

DRUEHE, Carl, from Hoexter; with Wilhelm THIELEMANN

ELSASSER, Ther(esia), from Teichensfeld; with Caroline BURKHARD & Jacob FRAENKEL

FABELMANN, Georg, from Altenburg

FLEMMING, Fr(iedrich), from Luebben

FRAENKEL, Jac(ob), from Teichensfeld; with Caroline BURKHARD & Theresia ELSASSER

FRASS, Conr(ad), from Stambach; with Christian THIEL

FRUGSESS? (TRUGSESS?), Joh(ann), from Ludwigsburg

GERSTENMEYER, Georg, from Kirchheim

GOEDING, Franz, from Luegde

GUTJAHR, H., from Holzthalleben; with wife

HANKEN, Juerg(en), from Lenstede

HERMSTAEDT, G. R., from Dresden

HIRSCHFELD, Emilie*, from Berlin

HUEBENER, Marg(arethe), from Coburg

HUGO, Henr(ich), from Hannover; with Johann HUGO & Dorothea BUCK

HUGO, Joh(ann), from Hannover; with Henrich HUGO & Dorothea BUCK

HUTZLER, Bab(ette?), from Hachenbach

JUNG, C. A., from Firnau

KESSEL, Anna, from Oberfuellbach; with family of 2 & Jacob BUECHNER & Georg ROSENBAUER

KETZER, H., from Nieste? (Rieste?)

KEYE, J. H. C., from Langeleben; with family of 4 & J. W. KEYE

KEYE, J. W., from Langeleben; with J. H. C. KEYE & family

KIRSCHENPFAD, Friedr(ich), from Heiligendorf

KNOBLAUCH, Carl, from Nuestadtgoedens

KNOPP, Friedr(ich), from Siedenburg

KOCH, Franz, from Braunschweig

KOERNER, Cath(arine), from Stotel

LANGGUTH, Dor(othea), from Koessfeld; with family of 2

LEMMRICH, Chr(istian), from Tambach; with Jacob BOHN

LIEBERMANN, Lor(enz?), from Rothenhof

LOEVINSOHN, Heinemann, place not given

MAEHLE, Chr(istian), from Osterode

MEYERHOFF, Ber(ends?), from Stotel

MOLDENHAUER, H., from Breslau

MUELLER, Andr(eas), from Lauterbach

MUELLER, Herm(ann) Th., from Altenburg; with H. DAUBERT, J. SCHUMANN, L. WIETE, & A. THEILIG

MUFF, J. G., from Geseel; with J. G. SCHREPPEL

NEUBRANDT, Mich(ael), from Steinau; with Dorothea SCHAEFER, & Joseph & Philippine SCHULTHEIS

PAULING, Joh(ann), from Allendorf

PIEPS, Fr(an)z, from Helmringhausen

RASSMANN, Cath(arine), from Burghausen

RINOW, Charl(es?), from Berlin; with family of 2 & Rudolph BAMANN & Rudolph SCHMIDT

ROMMEL, Joh(ann), from Hannover

ROSENBAUER, Georg, from Oberfuellbach; with Jacob BUECHNER & Anna KESSEL

ROTTNER, Solmar, from Zeitz

SAAYENGA, Carsten, from Larrelt; with 3 persons

SANDER, Gotth(ard?), from Heinzell

SCHAEFER, Dor(othea), from Steinau; with family of 2 & M. NEUBRANDT, Joseph & Philippine SCHULTHEIS

SCHATTING, Magd(alene), from Lauten; with Johann AUER & Margarethe SCHATTING

SCHATTING, Marg(arethe), from Lauten; with Johann AUER & Magdalene SCHATTING

SCHMIDT, Rud(olph), from Berlin; with Rudolph BAMANN & Charles RINOW

SCHOLL, Aug(ust), from Langensalza

SCHREPPEL, J. G., from Gesell; with J. G. MUFF

SCHULTHEIS, Jos(eph), from Steinau; with Philippine SCHULTHEIS, Dorothea SCHAEFER, & M. NEUBRANDT

SCHULTHEIS, Philippine, from Steinau; with Joseph SCHULTHEIS, Dorothea SCHAEFER, & Michael NEUBRANDT

SCHUMANN, Joh(ann), from Altenburg; with H. DAUBERT, L. WIETE, H. T. MUELLER, & A. THEILIG

SEILWOLD, Andr(eas), from Marktreig

THEILIG, Ant(on), from Altenburg; with H. DAUBERT, J. SCHUMANN, & L. WlETE, & H. T. MUELLER

THIEL, Chr(istian), from Stambach; with Conrad FRASS

THIELEMANN, W(ilhel)m, from Hoexter; with Carl DRUEHE

TIPPE, Lina, from Braunschweig

TROCKENBRODT. See TRUCKENBRODT

TRUCKENBRODT, Anna, from Wiesenfeld; with family of 2

TRUGSESS? (FRUGSESS?), Joh(ann), from Ludwigsburg

VOLLMER, --, widow, from Wetter

WALPER, Conr(ad), from Braunhausen; with family of 6

WALTHER, Erasmus, from Koerner; with B. C. DIETZ

WEDEL, Mart(in), from Mendhausen; with family of 6

WIETE, Louis, from Altenburg; with H. DAUBERT, J. SCHUMANN, H. T. MUELLER, & A. THEILIG

ZOEBISCH, Aug(ust), from Johanngeorgenstadt; with Natalie

ZOEBISCH, Natalie, from Johanngeorgenstadt; with August

List 7
Ship: Ocean Queen
Captain: -- Schoof
Departure Date: 24 Aug 1850
From: Bremen
To: New Orleans
Passengers: First Class, 10 persons; Steerage & Be-
tween-Deck, 295, including 12 babies
Citation: AAZ 4:103:411

BAETTGER, M., from Juda

BAHRUTH, H. N., from Ruetzebuettel; with family of 6

BARTELS, H., from Braunschweig; with family of 5

BECKMANN, G., from Neuenkirchen; with others

BERNHARD, M., from Zlabings

BIERHORST, J., from Dahlinghausen; with family of 4 & others

BIERSCHMALE, C., from Bockenem; with family of 4

BOEHNER, L., from Dinklage

BRASCH, H., from Wolfenbuettel

BROCKHAUS, H. A., from Lengerich; with others

BROCKSER, W., from Neuss; with Clemens ZERRES

BUECHSENSCHUETZ, G., from Torsitter; with family of 3

CHARGE, P., from Kaiserswerth; with P. ECHTENBROCH & Johann JAEGER

DASSLER, J. G., from Friesnitz; with family of 2

DIERKING, F., from Rodewald

DOHMEN, H., from New Orleans; with J. DOHMEN

DOHMEN, J., from New Orleans; with H. DOHMEN

DUERGES, C., from Bockenem; with W. STIGNOTH & A. KUENECKEN

ECHTENBROCH, P., from Kaiserswerth; with P. CHARGE & J. JAEGER

ECKHOLD, H. A., from Stadtilm; with A. JAHN, -- GER-STENBERGER, & J. N. REISLAND

FISCHER, E., from Culmbach; with J. PISTOR

FLOHR, J., from Gr(oss) Elbe; with family of 7 & C. HASE

FORKEL, S., from Coburg

FRANZES, A., from Lengerich; with others

FRICKE, A., from Lengerich; with others

FRIEDERICHS, F., from Timmelsen; with family of 4

FRUECHTING, D., from Mehren; with family of 2

GAETJEN, M. E., from Goldenstaedt; with F. THIECKE

GERSTENBERGER, --, widow, from Stadtilm; with family of 3 & A. JAHN, H. A. ECKHOLD, & J. REISLAND

GRAEF, C., from Lurich; with family of 2

HAAR, B. H. v(on) d(er), from Lengerich; with others

HASE, C., from Gr(oss) Elbe; with J. FLOHR

HEISE, H. F., from Tennstaedt; with family of 5

HENZE, C., from Bissingsleben; with family of 3

HERZ, R., from Zarachemo; with S. HERZ

HERZ, S., from Zarachemo; with R. HERZ

HESS, C., from Crenzburg; with family of 2

HILLUNG, H., from Hordinghausen; with H. WEBER

HINRIKS, M., from Dahlinghausen; with others

HOERSCHGEN, H., from Buederich; with family of 6

HOTHO, J., from Roedinghausen; with C. NIEDERFELD

HUEPER, G., from Varel; with family of 4

HUETER, C., from Bockenem; with W. HUETER & J. H. KRUEGER

HUETER, W., from Bockenem; with C. HUETER & J. H. KRUEGER

HUTMACHER, C., from Kaarst

JABIN, J., from Kelbra; with family ot 2 & L. VOLLMANN

JACOB, B., from Lengerich; with others

JAEGER, Joh(ann), from Kaiserswerth; with P. ECHTENBROCH & J. CHARGE

JAHN, A., from Stadtilm; with -- GERSTENBERGER, H. A. ECKHOLD, & J. N. REISLAND

JANSEN, W., from Erfurt; with L. SCHNEIDER

KAESTNER, F., trom Gruessen; with J. KAESTNER

KAESTNER, J., from Gruessen; with F. KAESTNER

KALKER, M., from Bockum

KAUERTZ, Joh(ann), trom Linn

KESSLER, H., from Bremen

KLAUBER, A., from Dasslof

KLUENER, W., from Langist; with family of 5

KNIPPENBERG, M., from Dahlinghausen; with family of 2 & others

KOEBBE, J. C., from Lengerich

KOEBLITZ, J.,

KOEHNEN, C., from Kaiserswerth; with M. KOEHNEN

KOEHNEN, M., from Kaiserswerth; with C. KOEHNEN

KREMER, Jac(ob), from Creteld; with tamily of 3

KRUEGER, J. H., from Bockenem; with C. & W. HUETER

KRUSEN, Meta*, from Lessum

KUEHLMANN, H., from Linn; with Joseph STAPPER

KUENECKEN, A., from Bockenem; with family ot 2 & W. STIGNOTH & C. DUERGES

LAHMANN, W., from Neuenkirchen; with others

LANGGUTH, --, from Brallendorf

LAVRENZ? (LAURENZ?), P., from Schleswig

LEINKER, B., from Dahlinghausen; with others

LES, B., from Lengerich; with others

LEVERKEN, H., from Weichels

LINDNER, A. E., from Roth; with C. L. LINDNER

LINDNER, C. L., from Roth: from A. E. LINDNER

LOECKENHOF, G., from Grundbach

MAGERS, F., from Wulfladen

MENCKE, T., from Lengerich; with others

MEYER, F., from Liensburg

MEYER, M. A., from Lengerich; with others

MEYER, M. A., with tamily of 8 & others

MUELLER, F., from Friedrichsbrunn

NEGROTT, A., from Hatten; with family of 2

NIEDERFELD, C., trom Roedinghausen; with family of 6 & J. HOTHO

OBERHAUPT, Gertr(ude), from Ilverich; with Jacob WESERS, -- PORTH, & Paul SCHMITZ

OBERSCHORFHEIDE, H., from Neuenkirchen; with H. SCHORFHEIDE

PATTHOF, H., from Neuenkirchen; with others

PERGER, Ferd(inand)*, from Altenburg; with Julius PERGER & F. E. POECHEL

PERGER, Jul(ius?)*, from Altenburg; with Ferdinand PERGER & F. E. POECHEL

PFEIL, Jos(eph), trom Kalkum; with family of 8 & August SCHMITZ

PISTOR, J., trom Culmbach; with E. FISCHER

POECHEL, F. E.*, from Altenburg; with Julius & Ferdinand PERGER

POEVGES? (POEPGES?), W., from Suechteln

PORTH, --, widow, from Ilverich; with family of 4 & J. WESERS, G. OBERHAUPT, & P. SCHMITZ

PRASSE, R., trom Osnabrueck; with W. SCHOLLER & B. RAMMERT

PUESCHKE, G., from Breslau

PUETZ, W(ilhel)m, from Buederich; with family of 6

RAHMEL, T., trom Heigerthal; with C. STEIGERDAHL

RAMMERT, B., from Osnabrueck; with W. SCHOLLER & R. PRASSE

RAMPENDAHL, F., from Henne; with C. WIESE

REISLAND, J. N., from Stadtilm; with A. JAHN, -- GERSTENBERGER, & H. A. ECKHOLD

RESE, J. H., from Carnau; with family of 4

RIECKE, H., from Neuenkirchen; with others

ROEHR, F(ran)z, from Muenster; with Georg SCHONNEBECK

ROSE, --, Mrs., from Detmold; with family of 6

RUETGERS, R., from Sirm

SCHILLING, M., trom Grimlinghausen

SCHLUMP, A. M., from Lengerich; with others

SCHMITZ, Aug(ust), from Kalkum; with Joseph PFEIL

SCHMITZ, C. J., from Duesseldorf

SCHMITZ, J. P., from Nierst; with family of 5

SCHMITZ, Paul, from Ilverich; with -- PORTH, Jacob
WESERS, & Gertrude OBERHAUPT

SCHNEIDER, L., from Erfurt; with W. JANSEN

SCHOLLER, W., from Osnabrueck; with B. RAMMERT & R.
PRASSE

SCHONNEBECK, Georg, from Muenster; with Franz ROEHR

SCHORFHEIDE, H., from Neuenkirchen; with H. OBER-
SCHORFHEIDE

SCHROEDER, A. M., from Lengerich; with H. SCHROEDER &
others

SCHROEDER, H., from Lengerich; with A. M. SCHROEDER &
others

SCHULTZE, H., from Neuenkirchen; with others

SCHUMACHER, A. M., from Lengerich; with others

SCHWALENSTECKLER, G., from Bastorf; with family of 3

SCHWARZ, A., from Angermunde

SCHWARZENBACH, H., from Waldenschweil

SCHWARZENBACH, J. J.*, from Waldenschweil

SCHWETHELM, E., from Struemp; with family of 3

SIMEON, W(ilhel)m, from Herzberg

SOELNER, B., from Sauerhof

STAPENBRINK, C., from Neuenkirchen; with others

STAPPER, Jos(eph), from Linn; with family of 12 & H.
KUEHLMANN

STEIGERDAHL, C., from Heigerthal; with T. RAHMEL

STEIN, F., from Oberomen

STIGNOTH, W., from Bockenem; with family of 3 & C.
DUERGES, & A. KUENECKEN

STOHLMANN, M., from Dahlinghausen; with others

TEHLEN, B., from Lengerich; with others

THIECKE, F., from Goldenstaedt; with M. E. GAETJEN

UTHE, C., from Hohlstedt

VELTFORT, J. H., from Quackenbrueck; with family of 3

VOLLMANN, L., from Kelbra; with family of 4 & J. JABIN

VON DER HAAR, B. H. See B. H. v. d. HAAR

WEBER, H., from Hordinghausen; with H. HILLUNG

WEGGANG, A., from Nordwalde; with family of 3

WESERS, Jac(ob), from Ilverich; with -- PORTH, Gertrude OBERHAUPT, & Paul SCHMITZ

WETZLICH, E. A., from Schoenborn

WICHLER, Louis, from Reuss

WIEGMANN, J. H. C., from Liebenau

WIESE, C., from Henne; with F. RAMPENDAHL

WILHELM, G., from Rohden

WILKEN, D., from New Orleans

WILKENS, Mad(am?) or Madeline?)*, from Bremen; with 2
daughters

ZEITSCHEL, Charles*, from New Orleans; with wife

ZERRES, Clemens, from Neuss; with W. BROCKSER

ZINSER, --, widow; from Schotten

ZONS, M., from Lank

List 8
Ship: **President Smidt**
Captain: -- Meyer
Departure Date: 19 Sep 1850
From: Bremen
To: New Orleans
Passengers: First Class, 12 persons; Second Class,
Steerage & Between-Deck: 221 persons
Citation: AAZ, 4:116:463

AMSCHLER, J. G., from Moenchau; with S. F. TAEUBER &
F. HAHN

BACKHAUS, M., from Spreda

BEHNER, M., from Doeberschutz

BEHNER, M. B., from Wirnsreuth; with family of 2 & E.
STROBEL

BEINDORFF, Carl*, from Varel

BINDEMEYER, B., from Bakum; with B. JOHANNES & B. KATH-
MANN

BIRNSTEIN, Aug(ust), from Braenau

BLASE, Fr(iedrich), from Werther

BOART, H., from Stemmen; with others

BOLIVAR, P., from Horn; with C. LOHME & S. HELLE

BREIER, C., from Kutenhausen

BRINKMANN, B., from Varenholz; with H. VENNEKOHL

BRUEGGEMANN, E. H., from Belm; with family of 5

BUEHRMANN, H. H., from Luehrte; with family of 3

BUERGER, Fr(ie)d(ri)ke*, from Detmold

BUSCHMEIER, F., from Rehme? (Nehme?)

CARSTENS, H. C.*, from Broekhave

CONRADES, H., from Liebenau

CORDESMANN, A. M., from Langfoerden; with others

DIPPOLD, J., from *angenstadt; with family of 6

DOHRMANN, F. W.*, from Bremen

DRESSENDOERFER, E., from Dondorf

ELBRACHT, M., from Brokhagen; with family of 2 & -- KOMBRINK

FASCHEN, --, widow, from Kalbslage; with family of 3

FISCHER, E., from Elbrinksen; with W. & S. SCHAEFER & D. RAECKER? (NAECKER?)

FOBUSCH, Julie*, from Engter; with Louis

FOBUSCH, Louis*, from Engter; with Julie

FOCKE, H., from Bremen

FUCHS, C., from Baireuth

GEMKE, M., from Borgholzhausen; with L. NIEHAUS

GIFHORN, Fr(iedrich), from Salzgitter

HAHN, F., from Moenchau; with family of 3 & S. F. TAEUBER & J. G. AMSCHLER

HAUEN, S., from Stemmen; with others

HAUPT, G., from Sindlingen

HEIDKAMP, F., from Borhholzhausen; with others

HELLE, S., from Horn; with C. LOHME & P. BOLIVAR

HELLE, S. H., from Horn; with H. SCHIERENBERG

HINNERS, H., from Thoelstedt; with family of 6

HIRSCHMANN, C., from Leineck; with family of 4

HOFFMANN, --*, from Coburg; with family of 4

HOLTMEIER, M. E., from Haltern; with A. M. KREYENHAGEN

HORETH, Anna Cath(arine), from Aichig; with Kunigunde & Barbara

HORETH, Barb(ara), from Aichig; with Kunigunde & Anna Catharine

HORETH, J., from Eichelberg; with Kunigunde, Anna Catharine, & Barbara

HORETH, Kunig(unde), from Aichig; with Anna Catharine, Barbara, & J. HORETH

HORTHER, E., from Wiesenfels

HUSEN, J. v(on), from Vechta

IKEN, Herm(ann)*, from Bremen

JOHANNES, B., from Bakum; with B. BINDENMEYER & B. KATHMANN

KAISER, F., from Langenholzhausen; with family of 3

KATHMANN, B., from Bakum; with B. JOHANNES & B. BINDE-MEYER

KEIL, A., from Neukirchen

KELBE, H., from Schlangen

KELLER, S., from Bodenmuehle

KLOEPPER, H., from Kutenhausen

KOCH, Mar(garethe?), from Siedenburg

KOMBRINK, --, Mrs., from Brokhagen; with family of 3 & M. ELBRACHT

KORTLANK? (KORTLAUK?), C., from Hohenhausen

KRAEMERS, --, widow, from Borgholzhausen; with others

KREYENHAGEN, A. M., from Haltern; with M. E. HOLTMEIER

KROPF, J. G., from Thurnau; with family of 7

KUNHOLZ, L., from Borgholzhausen; with others

LANGENBERG? (LAUGENBERG?), W., from Borgholzhausen; with others

LAUGENBERG? (LANGENBERG?), W., from Borgholzhausen; with others

LIENEMANN, A., from Engter; with M. LIENEMANN

LIENEMANN, M., from Engter; with A. LIENEMANN

LOHME, C., from Horn; with S. HELLE & P. BOLIVAR

LUEHRS, D., from Holtrup

LUEUELF, A., from Stemmen; with W. LUEUELF & others

LUEUELF, W., from Stemmen; with A. LUEUELF & others

MENDELSOHN, D., from Ovelgoenne; with E. MENDELSOHN

MENDELSOHN, E., from Ovelgoenne; with D. MENDELSOHN

MEYER, H., from Kutenhausen; with family of 6 & C. ROHLFING? (NOHLSING?)

MEYER, L., from Brokhagen

MUELLER, C., from Wietersheim

MUELLER, Clara*, from Meiningen

NAECKER? (RAECKER?), D., from Elbrinksen; with W. & S. SCHAEFER & E. FISCHER

NAHTERS? (RAHTERS?), M., from Todtenhausen

NEUHAUS, Hr. (Heinrich?), from Bremen

NIEHAUS, L., from Borgholzhausen; with M. GEMKE

NOHLSING? (ROHLFING?), C., from Kutenhausen; with H. MEYER

NOLTE, W., from Stemmen; with family of 7 & others

NUETZEL? (RUETZEL?), J., from Bindlach

OFFER, A., from Borgholzhausen; with others

OPPERMANN, C., from Vorweke

OTT, C., from Baireuth

PRIOHR, G. H., from Graevinghausen

PUNDT, B., from Langfoerden; with others

RAAB, E., from Baireuth

RAECKER? (NAECKER?), D., from Elbrinksen; with W. & S. SCHAEFER & E. FISCHER

RAHTERS? (NAHTERS?), M., from Todtenhausen

RAPS, J., from Wolfsbach

RICKER, F., from Bendorf; with W. RICKER, & M. & S. RIDDER

RICKER, W., from Bendor; with family of 4 & F. RICKER & M. & S. RIDDER

RIDDER, M., from Bendorf; with S. RIDDER & others

RIDDER, S., from Bendorf; with M. RIDDER & others

RIGGE, W., from Bendorf; with family of 5 & others

ROHLFING? (NOHLSING?), C., from Kutenhausen; with H. MEYER

RUETHER, Anna M., from Borgholzhausen; with others

RUETZEL? (NUETZEL), J., from Bindlach

SANDERS, A., from Wildeshausen

SCHAEFER, S., from Elbrinksen; with W. SCHAEFER, E. FISCHER, & D. RAECKER? (NAECKER?)

SCHAEFER, W., from Elbrinksen; with S. SCHAEFER, E. FISCHER, & D. RAECKER? (NAECKER?)

SCHIERENBERG, H., from Horn; with family of 5 & S. H. HELLE

SCHILLMUELLER, A., from Langfoerden; with others

SCHMAEDES, M., from Langfoerden; with others

SCHMIDT, H., from Stemmen; with family of 7 & others

SCHMIDT, J. S., from Hutschdorf

SCHRADER, Fr(iedrich), from Breistadt; with H. STAATS

SCHUMACHER, Matth(ias)*, from New Orleans

SIEKMANN, C., from Bendorf; with others

SIEKMANN, F., from Stemmen; with family of 6 & others

STAATS, H., from Breistedt; with Friedrich SCHRADER

STROBEL, E., from Wirnsreuth; with family of 2 & M. B. BEHNER

SUEDBECK, J., from Kalbslage

SUTHOF, M. E., from Darum; with family of 2

TAEUBER, S. F., from Moenchau; with F. HAHN & J. G. AMSCHLER

TOELLE, Anna M., from Borgholzhausen

V(on) HUSEN, J., from Vechta

VENNEKOHL, H., from Varenholz; with family of 4 & B. BRINKMANN

VOGT, F. W., from Borgholzhausen; with family of 6 & others

WAEHRMANN, L., from Vechta

WEIERMUELLER, K., from Dondorf

WELKENER, M. E., from Eggermannskotten

WENDELER, E., from Dielingen

WENDT, Anna Adelh(eid?), from Neudorff

WENTE, L., from Bakum

WENZEL, F., from Neundorf; with H. WENZEL

WENZEL, H., from Neundorf; with F. WENZEL

WIEKEMAKER, A., from Damme

WILKER, G. H., from Pome? (Bome?)

WIELENBROOK, L., from Langfoerden; with others

WINDEKER, Jac(ob)*, from Wildeshausen; with wife

ZIEBEL, --, from Bremerhaven

List 9
Ship: Estafette
Captain: -- Heyen
Departure Date: 19 Sep 1850
From: Bremen
To: Galveston
Passengers: 58 persons
Citation: AAZ 4:116:463
Note: Thirty-five of the passengers listed below [those from the villages of Neufilzen, Muelheim, Dusemond, Irmenach, Obercostenz, & Belch] in the Mosel region were accompanied to Bremen by their travel agent F. W. Geilhausen of Coblenz. They expressed their gratitude to him for his services.

ALBERTHAL, A., from Belch; with family of 4

BAUM, A., from Obercostenz; with others

BELTEN, H., from Obercostenz; with family of 4, Jacob BELTEN, & others

BELTEN, Jac(ob), from Obercostenz; with H. BELTEN & others

BERNDT, E., from Schweidnitz; with W. EINKAUF & C. SCHMIDT

BRODT, N., from Ostheim

EBERHARD, W., from Winzlar; with family of 2 & F. HOERMANN

EINKAUF, W., from Schweidnitz; with family of 4 & C. SCHMIDT & E. BERNDT

ERASMUS, C. F., from Straßsund; with family of 2

ERLER, H., from Lokenwalde

FATSCH, J. W., from Irmenach; with N. FATSCH & others

FATSCH, N? (R?), from Irmenach; with J. W. FATSCH & others

GINDORF, S., from Dusemond

GOLD, W., from Obercostenz; with family of 6 & others

HOERMANN, F., from Winzlar; with family of 6 & W. EBERHARD

KIESER, Cath(arine), from Muelheim; with Franz KIESER

KIESER, F(ran)z, from Muelheim; with Catharine KIESER

LORENZ, A., from Irmenach; with others

OCHS, Nic(olaus), from Irmenach; with family of 4 & others

RODENBUSCH, A., from Obercostenz; with family of 4 & others

SANTER, C., from Diepoldshofen

SCHAEFER, J., from Raboldshausen

SCHMIDT, C., from Schweidnitz; with W. EINKAUF & E. BERNDT

SCHMIDT, D. H., from Lehmden

SCHNEIDER, W., from Irmenach; with others

SCHUMACHER, M., from Rosdorf; with family of 2

THOMAS, Nic(olaus), from Neufilzen; with family of 4

List 10
Ship: Ammerland (Oldenburg flag)
Captain: -- Fehrs
Departure Date: 20 Sep 1850
From: Bremen
To: New York
Passengers: 170 persons
Citation: AAZ, 4:116:463

ARGUS, C. G., from Greitz

BAUMHOEFER, M., from Westbarkhausen

BECK, C., from Fresco; with J. LINZNER

BERTHOLD, C., from Leipzig

BEU, F., from Neuhaus

BOEDEKER, J., from Bergheim

BOLT, A., from Bueckeburg; with H. BOLT & -- RIETMEYER

BOLT, H., from Bueckeburg; with A. BOLT & -- RIETMEYER

BOSSE, C., from Burgdorf

BRACKENSIEK? (BRACKENFIEK?), P. H., from Riemsloh; with family of 6

BROEHERMANN, A. M., from Hunteburg; with J. F. BROEHERMANN

BROEHERMANN, J. F., from Hunteburg; with A. M. BROEHERMANN

BRUENING, J. H., from Bentheim; with family of 4

BUEHLER, J. G., from Philippsburg

CLAUSEN, H. G., from Brake

DEGERING, C., from Clausthal

DEWENTER, A., from Rohde; with F. DEWENTER, F. & A. DIERKES, & H. HILLE

DEWENTER, F., from Rohde; with A. DEWENTER, F. & A. DIERKES, & H. HILLE

DIERKES, A., from Rohde; with F. DIERKES, A. & F. DEWENTER, & H. HILLE

DIERKES, F., from Rohde; with A. DIERKES, A. & F. DEWENTER, & H. HILLE

DITTMAR, J., from Rudlar; with G. HOFFMANN & J. HENKEL

DONAU, C., from Bremen

DOSSING, J., from Schwabach

ECKARDT, J., from Leimbach; with J. G. & J. SCHUEDRUMPF

EICHMANN, W., from Ostercappeln; with C. SCHLIEPER

FISCHER, E., from Ankum; with H. FISCHER & J. H. REHMELMANN? (NEHMELMANN?)

FISCHER, F., from Breslau

FISCHER, H., from Ankum; with E. FISCHER & J. H. REHMELMANN? (NEHMELMANN?)

FOERG, Matth(ias), from Hankofen; with Theresia & Walbert

FOERG, Ther(esia), from Hankofen; with Matthias & Walbert

FOERG, Walb(ert?), from Hankofen; with Matthias & Theresia

FORCHTEL, J., from Altdorf

FRERICHS, H., from Nartmoor

GERLACH, F., from Landershausen

GROHNE, J., from Wuergasen; with H. HENNING & S. WREDE

GROTHE, H., from Wambeck

GUENTHER, J., from Binsebeck

HAEMLEIN, C., from Kingsey

HARTWIG, A., from Rothenkirchen

HENKEL, J., from Rudlar; with family of 2 & G. HOFF-
    MANN & J. DITTMAR

HENNING, H., from Wuergasen; with J. GROHNE & S. WREDE

HILLE, H., from Rohde; with A. & F. DEWENTER, F. & A.
    DIERKES

HOFFMANN, G., from Rudlar; with J. DITTMAR & J. HENKEL

HOHN, M., from Kadnitz; with family of 3

HOPPE, H., from Natzum

JAEGER, G., from Kleinenseen; with family of 3

JOELLENBECK, W., from Neuenkirchen

KAEHRING, L., from Beller

KAMLACH, C., from Halle

KAUFHOLD, C., from Uder

KLAAS, H., from Sabenhausen; with family of 6

KLOTZ, G., from Berlin; with F. STUEBEN

KOPPEL, H., from Lessum; with family of 6

KRAMER, L., from Biedenkopf; with family of 3

KRITTELBACH, H., from Ochstadt

KUEFNER, J., from Neudorf

LINZNER, J., from Fresco; with C. BECK

LOHMANN, L., from Dielingen

LUECKMANN, H., from Lastrup

MEYBECK?, B., from Oelde; with G. ROLDENBURG & O. F.
    UETEN

MEYER, F., from Soegeln; with family of 4

MEYER, H., from Erfurt

MOCK, W., from Niederrothenbach

MOSHEIM, M., from Springe

NEHMELMANN? (REHMELMANN?), J. H., from Ankum; with H.
    & E. FISCHER

NEST? (REST?), S., from Herstelle

NOLDENBURG? (ROLDENBURG?), G., from Oelde; with B.
    MEYBECK & O. F. UETEN

NOLTE, F., from Herstelle; with family of 3 & F. WIL-
    MAR

OSMERS, H., from Ballen

PETTINGER, F., from Ettling

RAABE, --, from Heimershausen; with family of 3

REHMELMANN? (NEHMELMANN?), J. H., from Ankum; with H.
    & E. FISCHER

REST? (NEST?), S., from Herstelle

RHODE, H., from Sickerode; with family of 5

RIEPE, H., from Powe; with family of 4

RIETMEYER, --, from Bueckeburg; with H. BOLT

RITTER, C., from Coburg

ROBERTS, H. L., from Hannover

ROLDENBURG? (NOLDENBURG?), G., from Oelde; with B.
    MEYBECK & O. F. UETEN

ROLF, A., from Itter? (Ikker?)

ROTH, S., from Neundorf

ROTHERMICH, J., from Obernburg

RUDLOFF, J., from Berka; with family of 4

RUGBACH, A., from Goslar

SAUER, E., from Zischen

SCHLIEPER, C., from Otercappeln; with W. EICHMANN

SCHLUETER, H., from Schwalenberg

SCHMIDT, F. M., from Niederzimmer

SCHRADER, W., from Dassensen

SCHROEDER, L., from Bergholzhausen

SCHUEDRUMPF, J., from Leimbach; with family of 3, J. G.
    SCHUEDRUMPF & J. ECKARDT

SCHUEDRUMPF, J. G., from Leimbach; with J. SCHUEDRUMPF
    & J. ECKARDT

SCHUETTE, --, widow; from Hameln

SCHULTHEIS, G. M., from Coburg

SCHWARBACH, c., from Achmer

SCHWEERS, D., from Bremen

SCHWEIGER, A., from Rockolding

STAHL, E., from Hersum; with family of 3

STAHLKNECHT, E., from Allendorf

STRAUBING, L., from Carlsruhe

STRUSS, H. H., from Badbergen

STUEBEN, F., from Berlin; with G. KLOTZ

STUENNE, A., from Biedenbach

TEBBE, C., from Wunstorf; with family of 4

TEWES, W., from Wuergasen; with -- ZERNITZ

TWISTE, A., from Herstelle

UETEN, O. F., from Oelde; with G. ROLDENBURG & B. MEY-BECK

WEBER, M., from Bulach

WELLMANN, W., from Sulingen

WOLTKE, A. A., from Loeningen; with family of 6

WREDE, S., from Wuergasen; with H. HENNING & J. GROHNE

ZERNITZ, --, widow, from Wuergasen; with family of 6 & W. TEWES

ZINN, G., from Farnoda

List 11
Ship: Reform
Captain: W. Hattendorf
Departure Date: 34(!) Oct 1850
From: Bremen
To: San Francisco
Passengers: 65 persons
Citation: AAZ 4:128:511

BOHLENS, Ed(uard), businessman, from Bremen

BREITENBACH, Franz, student, from Duderstadt

BRUENING, Fr(iedrich), miner, from Aachen; with F. M. LABRY

BUCHNER, Joh(ann), wood turner, from Mainz; with wife & Carl Joseph LEHNHARDT

CLAVITTER, Ed(uard), innkeeper, from San Francisco; with wife

CRESPY, Magnier de, pensioner (Rentier), from Stass-burg

FABRICIUS, Georg, businessman, from Koeln

FINK, Therese, from Warburg; with daughter

FRANKE, Auguste, from Bremen

GLEIM, Carl Friedrich, landowner, from San Francisco; with wife

GUDOPP, R., former Prussian lieutenant (Cuirassier), from Bromberg

HEIDTMAN, Maria, from Ottersberg

HEINEKEN, --, businessman, from Bremen (formerly in San Francisco)

HODES, Aug(ust), sailor, from Herstelle; with G. WUER-TEMBERG

HOLDE, Rebecca, from Hude

HOLL, Carl Friedrich, peasant, from Hohebach bei Kuenzelau

KOENIG, J. G., peasant, from Gehrde; with C. W. S. VOIGT

KOLLIGS, Albert, forester, from Duderstadt; with Joseph MALLART, Adolph WAGNER, & A. R. ZAHN

KOMPFF, Ferdinand, farmer, from Wiesbaden; son of Louis KOMPFF

KOMPFF, Louis, portrait painter, from Wiesbaden; with Theodor & Ferdinand (sons)

KOMPFF, Theod(or), farmer, from Wiesbaden; son of Louis KOMPFF

KUETHMANN, L. H., businessman, from Bremen

LABRY, F. M., machinist, from Aachen; with Friedrich BRUENING

LEHNHARDT, Carl Jos(eph), writer, from Mainz; with Johann BUCHNER

LENZ, H., businessman & former Prussian Artillery petty officer, from Bromberg

LEUW, G., farmer & businessman, from Cleve

LOERSCH, R., businessman, from Aachen

LOESCH, Elise, from Cassel

LUDOLLPH, H., machinist, from Klettbach; with wife

MALLART, Joseph, businessman, from Duderstadt; with Adolph WAGNER, Albert KOLLIGS, A. R. ZAHN

MAURER, Elise, from Carolinensiel; with Hermine

MAURER, Hermine, from Carolinensiel; with Elise

MESTER, Hermann, businessman, from Bremen

MUENSTER, Friederike, from Neustadt-Goedens; with family of 4; her husband sailed [to San Francisco] on same ship last year

NIEHE, Elise, from Neustadt-Goedens

PETERS, Elise, from Cassel

REICHHARDT, Anna Maria, Mrs., from Cassel; with daughter

REMSHARDT, F., tanner, from Heilbronn

RIEHN, C., miner & mine official, from Andreasberg

SCHENK, Fr(iedrich), wheelwright, from Lueneburg

SCHMIDT, Gustav, businessman, from Luebeck; with Reinhard ZAHN

SCHUETZ, H., official advisor (Referent) from Berlin

SCHWERIN, Count Hugo von, farmer, from Anclam; with Otto von SCHWERIN

SCHWERIN, Count Otto von, former Prussian lieutenant (Cuirassier), from Anclam; with Hugo von SCHWERIN

SOLDMANN, G. W. B., former Hanoverian Artillery lieutenant, from Coppenbruegge

STANGE, P. W., businessman, from Bremen

ULBRICH, Heinrich, mason, from Reichswaldau, Silesia

UNGAR, Leopold, businessman, from Bonn

VOIGT, C. W. S., baker & brewer, from Gehrde; with J. G. KOENIG

WAGNER, Adolph, bookbinder, from Duderstadt; with Joseph MALLART, Albert KOLLIGS, & A. R. ZAHN

WEDEMEYER, Louis, farmer, from Vlotho

WEIBLEN, C. W., businessman, from Reutlingen

WUERTEMBERG, G., businessman, from Herstelle; with August HODES

ZAHN, A. R., farmer, from Duderstadt; with Joseph MALLART, Adolph WAGNER, & Albert KOLLIGS

ZAHN, Heinr(ich), businessman, from Idstein

ZAHN, Reinh(ard or Reinhold), medical student, from Luebeck

List 12
Ship: Itzstein u. Welcker (three masts)
Captain: Heinrich Bosse
Departure Date: 27 Oct 1850
From: Bremen
To: New Orleans
Passengers: 254 persons
Citation: AAZ 4:137:547

AAR, von den. See VON DEN AAR

ABENDORFF, Diedr(ich), from Bremen; with Friedrich von BOKERN & Ernst Julius KEHRMANN

ARENDT, Chr(istian), from Heiligenstadt

BAHRMEISTER, Friedr(ich), from Hille; with family & others

BASSMANN, Cath(arine), from Alfhausen; with Ferdinand BASSMANN & others

BASSMANN, Ferd(inand), from Alfhausen; with Catharine & others

BAUMGARTEN, Joh(ann) Fr(iedrich), from Bremen; with G. Fr. KIRCHHOFF

BEEKMEYER, Friedr(ich), from Trier; with H. Wilhelm BEEKMEYER & others

BEEKMEYER, H. Wilh(elm), from Trier; with Friedrich BEEKMEYER & others

BEHREND, Friedr(ich), from Borgentreich; with Johann

BEHREND, Joh(ann), from Borgentreich; with Friedrich

BETKE, Cath(arine), from Alfhausen; with others

BODE, Friedr(ich) von, from Bergzabern

BOKEN, Elisab(eth) von, from Ankum; with Catharine FLASPOHLEN

BOKERN, Fr(iedrich) von, from Bremen; with Diedrich ABENDORFF & Ernst Julius KEHRMANN

BRINKER, H., from Wellingholzhausen; with family & Anna Elisabeth & Sophie MENGERS

BROCKHAUS, Bernh(ard), from Backerode; with family & Mar. Gesine BRUNS

BROCKHAUS, Herm(ann) Gerh(ard), from Ankum; with others

BROERMANN, H., from Ankum; with others

BRUEGGMANN, Cath(arine), from Hagen; with Johann BRUEGGMANN & others

BRUEGGMANN, Joh(ann), from Hagen; with Catharine BRUEGGMANN & others

BRUMWORD, C. H., from Hille; with others

BRUNNER, Joh(ann), from Muenchberg

BRUNS, Mar. Gesine, from Backerode; with Bernhard BROCKHAUS

BUETHMANN, Herm(ann) H., from Ankum; with others

BULTMANN, M. Elisab(eth), from Osnabrueck; with C. TONER, R. TOBERGK & C. WESER

DOESIUS, Friedr(ich), from Vogelbeck; with family & Friedrich GERBER & Louise KRUSE

DORMANN, Diedr(ich), from Bremen

EHLERS, Carl Fr(iedrich), from Bramsche

ERBST, Fried(rich), from Erbsen; with family & Mrs. -- GUENTHER

FLASPOHLEN, Cath(arine), from Ankum; with Elisabeth von BOKEN

FLORA, -- (siblings), from Husesel?; with Bertha KOHN

FRAMEYER, Cath(arine), from Hagen; with others

FREDE, G., from Bremen

FRESE, B. Heinr(ich), from Handrup; with family

GERBER, Fr(iedrich), from Vogelbeck; with Friedrich DOESIUS & Louise KRUSE

GERBIG, Marg(arethe), from Woifelden? (Wofelden?)

GERDES, Died(rich), from Alfhausen; with others

GERDING, Louise, from Hille; with Wilhelm GERDING & others

GERDING, Wilh(elm), from Hille; with Louise & others

GIFFMEYER, Cnarl(es), from Buer

GOEKE, Ant(on), from Rothe

GREWE, Joh(ann) M., from Borgloh; with family

GROSSEN, Fr(iedrich) W(ilhel)m, from S(ank)t Roda

GRUES, Herm(ann), from Lastrup; with others

GUENTHER, --, Mrs., from Erbsen; with family & Friedrich ERBST

HAANE? (HAGNE?), Friedr(ich), from Suedhemmern; with Elisabeth UPHOFF & Christian HORSTMANN

HEINEMANN, Heinr(ich), from Kemme

HENKE, Marie, from Elberfeld; with Friedrich HOBERG & Caroline STOMMEL

HENNECKE, Heinr(ich), from Altenaffeln; with family

HENSCHEN, Fr(iedrich) Wilh(elm), from Trier; with others

HOBERG, Fr(iedrich), from Elberfeld; with family & Marie HENKE & Caroline STOMMEL

HOPPE, H., from Hildesheim; with August SCHWERDT

HORSTMANN, Chr(istian), from Suedhemmern; with Elisabeth UPHOFF & Friedrich HAANE

HORSTMEIER, Wilh(elm), from Hille; with others

HUMMERT, B., from Ankum; with others

KALLSCHMIDT, Joh(ann) Fr(iedrich), from Trier; with others

KAMPMEYER, Gertr(ude), from Hagen; with others

KASSELMANN, Franz, from Hagen; with others

KASTEN, J. H. Z., from Hildesheim; with family

KAUFFOLD, Andr(eas), from Heiligenstadt; with Nicolaus KAUFFOLD & others

KAUFFOLD, Nic(olaus), from Heiligenstadt; with Andreas KAUFFOLD & others

KEHRMANN, Ernst Julius, from Bremen; with Diedrich ABENDORFF & Friedrich von BOKERN

KEMPER, Died(rich), from Ankum; with others

KERLS, Clemens, from Hoexter; with family

KETTENBRINK, Cath(arine), from Wellingshausen; with Clara Marie KETTENBRINK & Franz NEELMANN

KETTENBRINK, Clara Marie, from Wellingshausen; with Catharine KETTENBRINK & Franz NEELMANN

KIESEKAMP, F., from Bramsche

KIRCHHOFF, G. Fr(iedrich), from Bremen; with Johann Friedrich BAUMGARTEN

KLEIMEYER, Lina, from Hagen; with others

KOCH, Elisa(beth), from Ankum; with others

KOCK, Joh(ann), from Karmuetz

KOHN, Bertha, from Husesel?; with -- FLORA (siblings)

KONERSMANN, Elise, from Hagen; with others

KOTMANN, H., from Ankum; with others

KROCKMEYER, Wilh(elm), from Hille; with family & others

KROEGER, Ant(on), from Alfhausen; with others

KROEGER, Jos(eph), from Herzlake

KROGER, H., from Ankum; with others

KRUSE, Louise, from Vogelbeck; with Friedrich DOESIUS & Friedrich GERBER

KUCKUCK, G., from Dehmke

LAHR, H. von, from Ankum; with family & others

LAMPE, Joh(ann) Herm(ann), from Ankum; with others

LEMBECK, Bernh(ard), from Vinne; with family

LUEBBRECHT, Heinr(ich), from Wellingshausen; with others

LUEHRSEN, --, from Simmern

LUESSMANN, Maria, from Wellingshausen; with others

LUNGWITZ, Chr(istian) G., from Nauerheim? (Nauenheim?) with family

MARKWART, Balth(asar), from Wellingshausen; with others

MENGERS, Anna Elis(abeth), from Wellingshausen; with Sophie MENGERS & H. BRINKER

MENGERS, Sophie, from Wellingshausen; with Anna Elisabeth MENGERS & H. BRINKER

MEYER, Diedr(ich), from Hastedt

MEYER, Heinr(ich), from Leesering

MOEHLE, Chr(istian), from Hille; with others

MOELLER, Aug(ust), from Hildesheim

MOELLER, Christ(ian), from Seesen

MOHRMANN, Herm(ann), from Alfhausen; with family & others

MUELLER, Friedr(ich), from Feuchtwangen

NEELMANN, Franz, from Wellingshausen; with Clara Marie & Catharine KETTENBRINK

NIEBERG, H. Franz, from Melle

NIEMEYER, Christ(ian), from Hille; with family & others

NIENHUESER, Joh(ann) H., from Trier; with Mar. Elisabeth NIENHUESER & others

NIENHUESER, Mar. Elisab(eth), from Trier; with Johann H. NIENHUESER & others

NOLTING, Joh(ann) H., from Trier; with others

PEINE, Fritz, from Salzdetfurt

POHLMANN, Carl, from Hille; with others

PRIESHOFF, H., from Ankum; with others

REINECKE, Gottfr(ied), from Barrenrode; with family

ROTHERMUND, Werner, from Alfeld

SCHLINGER, Conr(ad), from Hille; with family & others

SCHLUETER, Friedr(ich), from Hille; with others

SCHLUETER, Luise, from Hille; with others

SCHMIDT, Henriette, from Stormbruch

SCHMUCK, Gertr(ude), from Alfhausen; with Hermann SCHMUCK & others

SCHMUCK, Herm(ann), from Alfhausen; with Gertrude SCHMUCK & others

SCHNEDLER, Ludw(ig), from Hille; with others

SCHULTE, Herm(ann), from Meppen; with Hermann Heinrich STEFFENS

SCHULTE, Peter, from Buehren; with family

SCHWARZ, Casp(ar) H., from Suedlingen; with family

SCHWERDT, Aug(ust), from Hildesheim; with H. Hoppe

SIEGENSTEIN, Franz, from Affeln; with family

SIEM, Christ(ian), from Skanderborg

SING, Christ(ian), from Heiligenstadt; with others

STALLMANN, Bernh(ard), from Alfhausen; with others

STARMANN, Elisab(eth), from Alfhausen; with H. STARMANN & others

STARMANN, H., from Alfhausen; with Elisabeth STARMANN & others

STEFFENS, Herm(ann) Heinr(ich), from Meppen; with Hermann SCHULTE

STEGEMANN, Ant(on), from Albachsen; with family

STIERLEIN, Louis, from Muenster; with wife & W. STIERLEIN

STIERLEIN, W., from Muenster; with Louis

STOMMEL, Caroline, from Elberfeld; with family & Friedrich HOBERG & Marie HENKE

TERHAGE, H., from Ankum; with others

THIELE, Alb., from Bremen

THIEMANN, W., from Hagen; with others

TIEMANN, Friedr(ich), from Hille; with others

TOBERGK, Rud(olph), from Osnabrueck; with Christine TORNER, Conrad WESER, & M. E. BULTMANN

TORNER, Christine, from Osnabrueck; with Rudolph TOBERGK, Conrad WESER, & M. E. BULTMANN

TUERMER, Jos(eph), from Heiligenstadt; with others

UPHOFF, Elisab(eth), from Suedhemmern; with family & Friedrich HAANE & Christian HORSTMANN

VON BODE, Friedrich, from Bergzabern

VON BOKEN, Elisab(eth), from Ankum; with Catharine FLASPOHLEN

VON BOKERN, Friedrich, from Bremen; with Diedrich MEYER & Ernst Julius KEHRMANN

VON DEN AAR, Caroline, from Hille; with Friederike VON DEN AAR & others

VON DEN AAR, Friederike, from Hille; with Caroline VON DEN AAR & others

VON LAHR, H., from Ankum; with family & others

VOSSE, Franz, from Wellingshausen; with others

VOSSSCHMIDT, David, from Trier; with others

WASSMANN, Carl, from Hille; with wife & others

WEHLAGE, Gertr(ude), from Alfhausen; with others

WELHAUSEN, H., from Ankum; with others

WELLBROCK, Joh(ann) Fr(iedrich), from Trier; with others

WESER, Conr(ad), from Osnabrueck; with family & C. TORNER, R. TOBERGK, & M. E. BULTMANN

WIEGE, Cath(arine), from Heiligenstadt; with others

WIESEBROCK, Joh(ann), from Verrel

WISKEN, Ludw(ig), from Alfhausen; with others

WITTE, Caroline, from Hildesheim

ZIMMERMANN, Ernst Fr(iedrich), from Leipzig

ZINGER, Joh(ann), from Heiligenstadt; with others

List 13
Ship: F. J. Wichelhausen (3 masts)
Captain: H. Warnken
Departure Date: 27 Oct 1850
From: Bremen
To: New Orleans
Passengers: 228 persons
Citation: AAZ 4:138:551

Note: Many of the relatives of passengers from Damme and Fladderlohhausen (or Fladderlohausen) who immigrated to the United States before 1850 are listed in Clifford Neal Smith, *Emigrants from the Former Amt Damme, Oldenburg (Now Niedersachsen), Germany, Mainly to the United States, 1830-1849.* German-American Genealogical Research Monograph Number 12 (McNeal, AZ: Westland Publications, 1981).

ALBERS, Addo, from Dietrichsfeld; with wife & Christian Friedrich WILMS

ALTHOFF, Anna Cath(arine), from Hecke; with family

BAUER, Marg(arethe), from Wohlmuthshuell; with family

BENKHOFF, Marg(arethe), from Epe; with others

BISSINGER, Isidor, from Gruol; with Elisabeth & Magdalene HEIZMANN

BOING, Herm(ann), from Epe; with others

BORSCHUETTMANN, Mar(cus? Martin?), from Fladderlohhausen; with others

BOSSBRINK, J. G., from Gehrde; with Johann H. GOYERT & others

BOWING, H., from Hennenkamp

BRAND, Carl, from Liebenau

BROCKMANN, Fr(iedrich), from Fladderlohhausen; with Friedrich KLEINE SEEPE

BRUNE, Elisab(eth), from Damme; with others

BUHRLAGE, Elisab(eth), from Damme; with others

BUSEKRUS, Cath(arine), from Valdorf; with family

CAMMERT, Chr(istian), from Gebhardsdorf

CHRIST, Andr(eas), from Biberach; with wife

DAMMING, Rudolph, from Epe; with family & others

DUERKOP, Doris, from Oldesloh

ESCHRICH, Chr(istian), from Maroldshausen

ESKEN, Cath(arine) Elisab(eth), from Fladderlohhausen; with others

FELDE, VOM. See VOM FELDE

FISCHER, Arnold, from Fladderlohhausen; with family

FOCKEN, S. Habbe; from Guemersum; with family

FREDE, G., from Vacha

FRYE, Gerd., from Fladderlohhausen; with others

FUCHS, Carl, from Pittsburg

GAERSE, Anna, from Laden; with Heinrich Wilhelm

GAERSE, Heinr(ich) Wilh(elm), from Laden; with Anna

GIESE, --, Mrs., from Rothefelde; with fami8y & Mrs. -- ZIMMERMANN

GOYERT, Joh(ann) H., from Gehrde; with J. G. BOSSBRINK & others

HABBE FOCKEN, S., from Guemersum; with family

HACKMANN, Engel, from Venne; with Heinrich

HACKMANN, Heinr(ich), from Venne; with Engel

HACKWART, Herm(ann), from Gross Wessum; with wife

HADLUNG, Marie, from Wimbach; with Adam RAUCH

HARKMEYER, H., from Damme; with family & others

HAUSFELD, Heinr(ich), from Fladderlohhausen; with family & others

HEDEBECK, Cath(arine), from Neuenkirchen; with Heinrich KLEIBECKER

HEIDE, VON DER, H., from Bergen

HEIZMANN, Elis(abeth), from Gruol; with Magdalene HEIZMANN & Isidor BISSINGER

HEIZMANN, Magd(alene), from Gruol; with Elizabeth HEIZMANN & Isidor BISSINGER

HELWIG, Cath(arine) Agnes, from Westercappeln; with Catharine Regine HELWIG & others

HELWIG, Cath(arine) Regine, from Westercappeln; with Catharine Agnes HELWIG & others

HEMPLER, Herm(ann), from Gehrde; with Gerhard STRUEVING

HERTER, Georg; from Savigny

HEYER, Herm(ann), from Ankum; with Catharine & Elisabeth VOM FELDE & Maria WESSLING

HOELZEL, MARG(arethe), from Buchenstein

HOLLE, Casp(ar) H., from Melle; with Johann Friedrich MEYER

HOLLMIG, August, from Ilverstedt; with Julius HOLLMIG

HOLLMIG, Julius, from Ilverstedt; with August HOLLMIG

HORNBACH, Joh(ann), from Zeudern

HUENEFELD, Anna Schulten, from Fladderlohhausen; with others

HUENEFELD, Joh(ann) G., from Fladderlohhausen; with others

HUGENBERG, H., from Ahe

IGELMANN, Elisab(eth), from Ahe

IMBUSCH, Heinr(ich), from Vechta; with wife

KAMMANN, Cath(arine) H., from Buende

KAUFMANN, Chr(istian), from Wermingshausen; with family

KITTLAGE, Heinr(ich), from Voerden; with Marie MOELL-
ENHOF, Christian MEYER, & H. STAHLBERG

KLEIBECKER, Heinr(ich), from Neuenkirchen; with Catharine HEDEBECK

KLEINE SEEPE, Friedr(ich), from Fladderlohhausen; with
Friedrich BROCKMANN & others

KOSIEG, Fr(iedrich), from Hardenberg

KUECK, Joh(ann), from Worpswed [so spelled]

LISKMANN, Wilk., from Iburg; with family & Theodor
RICHARD

LOEBNITZ, Herm(ann), from Naumburg

MAHNKE, Gebert, from Nordwede

MAHNKEN, Meta, from Meinertshagen

MARXMEYER, H., from Suedlanden

MENGEL, --, widow, from Mitterode; with family

MENKE, Heinr(ich), from Buchshorn; with family

MEYER, Christ(ian), from Voerden; with Marie MOELLEN-
HOF, Heinrich KITTLAGE, & H. STAHLBERG

MEYER, Heinr(ich), from Buende

MEYER, Joh(ann) Fr(iedrich), from Melle; with wife &
Caspar H. HOLLE

MEYLING, Joh(ann) H., from Gehrde; with family & Hermann WEISMANN & Heinrich MOHRMANN

MEYRING, Marg(arethe), from Epe; with Joseph ROHLING,
Gerhard WILMINK, & J. H. NIEHOF

MOELLENHOF, Marie, from Voerden; with Heinrich KITT-
LAGE, Christian MEYER, & H. STAHLBERG

MOHRMANN, Heinr(ich), from Gehrde; with Johann H. MEY-
LING, & Hermann WEISMANN

MUELLER, Friedr(ich), from Bibra

NIEHOF, J. H., from Epe; with Joseph ROHLING, Gerhard
WILMINK, & Margarethe MEYRING

OTTO, Heinr(ich), from Damme; with others

PETER, Georg, from Doernhagen

RABE, Engel, from Damme; with others

RAUCH, Adam, from Wimbach; with Marie HADLUNG

RICHARD, Theod(or), from Iburg; with Wilk. LISKMANN

RIEPERMANN, Anna M., from Haste; with family

RIESSKAMP, Juerg(en) H., from Westercappeln; with wife
& others

ROEMIGHE, Heinr(ich), from Wermingshaus; with family

ROHLING, Jos(eph), from Epe; with Gerhard WILMINK,
J. H. NIEHOF & Margarethe MEYRING

ROTTINGHAUS, Marie, from Damme; with others

RUDDE, Gerh(ard) Herm(ann), from Epe; with others

RUDELT, Carl Friedr(ich), from Luebeck; with family

SCHAEFER, Ludw(ig), from Bonneberg; with family

SCHILDKAMP, Elisab(eth), from Epe; with Marianne

SCHILDKAMP, Marianne, from Epe; with Elisabeth

SCHULTEN HUENEFELD, Anna, from Fladderlohhausen; with
others

SEEPE, Friedr(ich) Kleine, from Fladderlohhausen; with
Friedrich BROCKMANN

SOMMER, Herm(ann), from Altenbuellstadt; with family

STAHLBERG, Elisab(eth), from Voerden; with H. STAHL-
BERG, Marie MOELLENHOF, & others

STAHLBERG, H., from Voerden; with Elisabeth STAHLBERG,
Marie MOELLENHOF, & others

STANGIER, Joh(ann) Gerh(ard), from Coblenz; with wife

STRUEVING, Gerh(ard), from Gehrde; with wife & Hermann
HEMPLER

STUEHMEYER, Joh(ann) H., from Oberbecksen; with family

TEICHMANN, Heinr(ich), from Freiburg

THIROW, Carl, from Klein Lafferde; with family

TRIMPE, Heinr(ich), from Damme; with family & others

VOGLER, Carl, from Langenbilau; with family

VOM FELDE, Cat(arine), from Ankum; with Elisabeth VOM
FELDE & Hermann HEYER

VOM FELDE, Elisab(eth), from Ankum; with Catharine VOM
FELDE & Hermann HEYER

VON DER HEIDE, H., from Bergen

VOSS, H., from Hilter; with family

WALBRINK, Joh(ann) H., from Westercappeln; with others

WALDECKE, Jacob, from Cusel; with family

WEISMANN, Herm(ann), from Gehrde; with Johann H. MEY-
LING & Heinrich MOHRMANN

WERLING, Gerh(ard) H., from Epe; with family & others

WESSLING, Maria, from Ankum; with Hermann HEYER, Catharine & Elisabeth VOM FELDE

WIESENHAVERN, Friedr(ich) Gust(av), from Hildesheim

WIETE, Marie, from Damme; with others

WILKENING, Louis, from Heslingen

WILLEMBERG, Joseph, from Lemfoerde

WILMINK, Gerh(ard), from Epe; with Joseph ROHLING,
J. H. NIEHOF, & Margarethe MEYRING

WILMS, Chr(istian) Fr(iedrich), from Dietrichsfeld;

ZIMMERMANN, --, Mrs., from Rothenfelde; with Mrs. -- GIESE

ZITTERDING, N. N., from Fladderlohhausen; with others

List 14
Ship: Hudson (Bremen flag)
Captain: -- Hohorst
Arrival Date: 28 Nov 1850 on Weser [River]
From: New York
To: Bremen
Passengers: Cabin Class, 18 persons; Steerage: 35 persons
Citation: AAZ 4:150:599
Note: Although this list appears to be a trip back to Europe, it is valuable because places of origin (or trip destination?) are given.

ALBRECHT, Jory, from Meinholze

APPIASIUS, Heinrich, from Altenbruch

BLUME, Aug(ust), from Hildesheim; with 2 children & Thodor GROK

BOHLING, Claus, from Tarmenstedt

BONDY, Joseph*, from Prague, with 2 children & Jacob RAUDNITZ

DARNAUER, Herm(ann), from Westkilver

DELINGER, Ferd(inand), from Berlin

DOERINGBERGER, Carl, from Pensingen

DUENPEL, Anna Bab(ette?), nee TRUNG*, from Eisenach; with Christine DUENPEL

DUENPEL, Christine*, from Eisenach; with Anna Babette DUENPEL

FRANKEN. See Anna OHLWOE

FROEHLIG, Joh(ann), from Reipentenrode with Heinrich HARRIET

GALLE, Christ(ian), from Werfer

GERNET, Marg(arethe), from Fuerth

GRIEM, William B.*, from Eutien [now spelled Eutin]

GROK, Theo(dor), from Hildesheim; with August BLUME

HANSMANN, Carl*, from Ortens

HARLEING, Antoinette, nee HOEGG*, from Wuerzburg; with child

HARRIET, Heinr(ich), from Reipentenrode; with Johann FROEHLIG

HECKSTEDE, Mathilde, from Deggingen

HOEGG. See Antoinette HARLEING

HOLLWEDE, Christ(ian), from Loevern; with Theodor

HOLLWEDE, Theo(dor), from Loevern; with Christian

KLEKAMP, Joh(ann) H., from Dissen

KREINICK, Ant(on), from Amsterdam

KUEHN, Daniel, from Grossgalle

MARTH, Conr(ad), from Hilgerhausen

MEYER, Fr(ie)d(ri)ke, nee REMY*, from Cassel

MEYER, Heinr(ich), from Esdorf

MUELLER, Heinr(ich), from Lembro

NEBBE, Heinr(ich), from Weissenfels; with wife & 3 children

OHLWOE, Anna, nee FRANKEN*, from Wersabe

OMERBECK, Claus, from Bulling

RATH, Johanna, nee RIES*, from Wunsiedel, with child

RAUDNITZ, Jacob*, from Prague; with Joseph BONDY

REMY. See Friedrike MEYER

RIES. See Johanna RATH

RODENSTEIN, Diedr(ich), from Sundrach

SEILINGEN. See Eleonor STINGE

STEFFANY, Jos(eph), from Wuerzburg

STEIL, Herm(ann), from Meyenburg

STINGE, Eleon(or?), nee SEILINGEN, from Muenchen

TRUNG. See Anna Babette DUENPEL

WAGENFUEHRER, Adolph*, from Magdeburg

WASSERMANN, Heinr(ich), from Harpstedt

WEIGEL, Joh(ann)*, from Noedendorf? (Roedendorf?); with wife & child

WOELFER, Semann, from Erlangen

FRANZES, 7	GERSTENBERGER, 7	GROTE, 3	HARTMANN, 4
FRASS, 6	GERSTENMEYER, 6	GROTHE, 10	HARTWIG, 10
FREDE, 13	GIESE, 13	GRUES, 12	HASCH, ZUM, 1
FREDER, 12	GIESELMEYER, 1	GUDOPP, 11	HASE, 7
FREESE, 4	GIFFMEYER, 12	GUENTHER, 10, 12	HASENJAEGER, 1
FREIENSEENER, 5	GIFHORN, 8	GUETTICH, 3	HAU, 4
FRERICHS, 10	GILLE, 1	GUSMANN, 4	HAUEN, 8
FRESE, 12	GINDORF, 9	GUTJAHR, 6	HAUFF, 3
FREUND, 1	GLATZ, 4	GUTMANN, 1	HAUPT, 8
FREWER, 5	GLEIM, 11	GUTTENBERGER, 3	HAUSFELD, 13
FREYE, 5	GOEBEL, 1		HAUSMANN, 4
FRICKE, 7	GOEDING, 6	HAAN, de, 2	HAUSS, 3
FRIEDERICHS, 7	GOEKE, 1, 12	HAANE, 12	HEBBELER, 3
FRIEDRICH, 3	GOELLNER, 3	HAAR, VON DER, 7	HECKSTEDT, 14
FRIELING, 3	GOERTZ, 3	HAASE, 3	HEDEBECK, 13
FROEHLIG, 14	GOETZ, 4, 5	HABBE FOCKEN, 13	HEIDE, VON DER, 13
FROMM, 1	GOLD, 9	HACKMANN, 13	HEIDKAMP, 8
FRUECHTING, 7	GOLDBERG, 5	HACKWART, 13	HEIDTMAN, 11
FRUGSESS, 6	GOLDSCHMIDT, 3	HADLUNG, 13	HEIDTMANN, 4
FRYE, 13	GOPPELMANN, 1	HAEMLEIN, 10	HEIN, 5
FUCHS, 4, 5, 8, 13	GOTHMANN, 3	HAGNE, 12	HEINBUCH, 5
FURTMUELLER, 3	GOTTRALD, 5	HAHN, 3, 5, 8	HEINEKEN, 11
	GOYERT, 13	HAHNE, 1	HEINEMANN, 12
GADESMANN, 3	GRAEF, 5, 7	HALENBECK, 3	HEINFELD, 5
GAERSE, 13	GRAENICHER, 1	HALLENBERGER, 3	HEINLEIN, 5
GAETJEN, 7	GRAETZ, 4	HAMEL, 5	HEINZE, 3
GALLE, 14	GRAF, 5	HAMMERS, 2	HEISE, 7
GELHAUS, 5	GRESE, 1	HANHOFF, 1	HEIZMANN, 13
GEMKE, 8	GREWE, 12	HANKEN, 6	HELD, 5
GENER, 4	GRIEM, 14	HANSMANN, 14	HELLE, 8
GERBER, 12	GRIESELMANN, 1	HARBERT, 1	HELLER, 5
GERBIG, 12	GRIMMER, 5	HARKMEYER, 13	HELMKEN, 2
GERDES, 12	GROESCHNER, 1	HARLEING, 14	HELWIG, 13
GERDING, 12	GROHNE, 10	HARRIET, 14	HEMPLER, 13
GERLACH, 10	GROK, 14	HARTJE, 3	HENKE, 12
GERNET, 14	GROSSEN, 12	HARTKE, 1	HENKEL, 10

KITTLAGE, 13	KOMBRINK, 8	KUEFNER, 10	LINDNER, 7
KITZSTEINER, 4	KOMPFF, 11	KUEHLMANN, 7	LINZ, 1
KLAAS, 10	KONERSMANN, 12	KUEHN, 14	LINZNER, 10
KLAUBER, 7	KOPPEL, 10	KUENECKEN, 7	LISKMANN, 13
KLEIBECKER, 13	KORFF, 2	KUETHMANN, 11	LOEBNITZ, 13
KLEINE, 4	KORTEJOHANN, 4	KUNHOLZ, 8	LOECKENHOF, 7
KLEINE SEEPE, 13	KORTLANK, 8	KURZE, 4	LOEHEER, 5
KLEINMEYER, 12	KORTLAUK, 8	KUTZKY, 4	LOERSCH, 11
KLEKAMP, 14	KOSIEG, 13		LOESCH, 11
KLEPPEL, 5	KOTMANN, 12	LABRY, 11	LOEVINSOHN, 6
KLINGE, 3	KRAEMER, 1	LAHMANN, 7	LOEWE, 3
KLINGENSTEIN, 5	KRAEMERS, 8	LAHR, von, 12	LOHMANN, 10
KLIPP, 3	KRAMER, 1, 10	LAKEMANN, 2	LOHME, 8
KLOEPPER, 8	KRAUSE, 1	LAMPE, 12	LORENZ, 1, 9
KLOESS, 5	KRAUSS, 2, 5	LANGE, 4	LORIUS, 1
KLOTZ, 10	KREINICK, 14	LANGENBERG, 8	LUDOLLPH, 11
KLOTZBACH, 3	KREMER, 7	LANGGUTH, 6, 7	LUEBBRECHT, 12
KLUENER, 7	KRETZINGER, 5	LAUGENBERG, 8	LUECKMANN, 10
KLUGE, 3	KREYENHAGEN, 8	LAURENZ, 7	LUEDEKE, 5
KNAPP, 5	KRITTELBACH, 10	LAVRENZ, 7	LUEHRS, 3, 8
KNIPPENBERG, 7	KROCKMEYER, 12	LEBERMANN, 5	LUEHRSEN, 12
KNOBLAUCH, 6	KROEGER, 12	LEHNHARDT, 11	LUESSEN, 3
KNOPP, 6	KROELING, 3	LEINKER, 7	LUESSMANN, 12
KOATNER, 5	KROGER, 12	LEMBECK, 12	LUEUELF, 8
KOCH, 6, 8, 12	KRONER, 5	LEMMER, 3	LUNGWITZ, 12
KOCK, 12	KROPF, 8	LEMMRICH, 6	
KOEBBE, 7	KROPP, 3	LENZ, 5, 11	MACHELEDT, 1
KOEBLITZ, 7	KRUEGER, 5, 7	LEONHARDI, 3	MACKEROTH, 3
KOEHLER, 5	KRUHOEFFER, 3	LEPPERT, 4	MAEHLE, 6
KOEHNEN, 5, 7	KRUMM, 5	LES, 7	MAGD, 4
KOENIG, 11	KRUSE, 12	LEUW, 11	MAGERS, 7
KOERNER, 1, 6	KRUSEN, 7	LEVERKEN, 7	MAHNKE, 13
KOERTNER, 1	KUBISCH, 1	LIEBERMANN, 6	MAHNKEN, 13
KOHL, 4	KUCKUCK, 12	LIEBMANN, 1	MALEK, 3
KOHN, 12	KUEBLER, 4	LIENEMANN, 8	MALLART, 11
KOLLIGS, 11	KUECK, 13	LINDEMANN, 3	MANNEL, 3

MARDORF, 4

MARKWART, 12

MAROWSKY, 5

MARQUARDT, 2

MARST, 3

MARTH, 14

MARTINY, 1

MARWEDEL, 5

MARXMEYER, 13

MAURER, 11

MEHLIG, 1

MEHRTENS, 3

MEISTER, 5

MENCKE, 7

MENDEL, 5

MENDELSOHN, 8

MENGEL, 13

MENGERS, 12

MENGERT, 3

MENKE, 13

MENSING, 2

MESTER, 11

METTE, 5

METZGER, 5

MEYBECK, 10

MEYER, 1, 4, 7, 8, 10,
    12, 13, 14

MEYERHOFF, 6

MEYLING, 13

MEYRING, 13

MEYZEN, 4

MICHEL, 4

MOCK, 10

MOEHLE, 12

MOELLENHOF, 13

MOELLER, 4, 12

MOELLERS, 4

MOGK, 3, 5

MOHRMANN, 12, 13

MOLDENHAUER, 6

MOMBERGER, 5

MONTAG, 1

MOSHEIM, 10

MUELLER, 1, 2, 5, 6, 7, 8,
    12, 13, 14

MUENCH, 4, 5

MUENDER, 5

MUENSTER, 11

MUFF, 6

MULLER, 5

MURHARD, 4

MURTFELD, 3

MUTSCHLER, 4

NACHTIGALL, 3

NAECKER, 8

NAEMMLAEPP, 1

NAHTERS, 8

NEBBE, 14

NEELMANN, 12

NEGROTT, 7

NEHMELMANN, 10

NEST, 10

NEU, 5

NEUBAUER, 1

NEUBERT, 1

NEUBRANDT, 6

NEUHAUS, 8

NICOLAUS, 5

NIEBERG, 12

NIEDERFELD, 7

NIEHAUS, 8

NIEHE, 11

NIEHOF, 4, 13

NIEMANN, 3, 5

NIEMEYER, 12

NIENHUESER, 12

NITSCHE, 4

NOHLSING, 8

NOLDENBURG, 10

NOLL, 4

NOLTE, 8, 10

NOLTENIUS, 3

NOLTING, 1, 12

NOMMINGER, 4

NUETZEL, 8

OBERHAUPT, 7

OBERSCHORFHEIDE, 7

OCHS, 9

OENECK, 4

OETERS, 3

OFFER, 8

OHLDEMEYER, 2

OHLWOE, 14

OMERBECK, 14

OPPERMANN, 8

OSMERS, 10

OSTER, 1

OTT, 8

OTTO, 4, 13

PALGEMEYER, 5

PATTHOF, 7

PAULING, 6

PAUSSE, 4

PEINE, 12

PERGER, 7

PETER, 13

PETERS, 3, 11

PETTINGER, 10

PETZ, 5

PFAHLER, 3

PFEIFFER, 3

PFEIL, 7

PIEPS, 6

PINGEL, 1

PISTOR, 7

PLAHT, 1

PLOEGER, 3

PLUMHOFF, 1

POECHEL, 7

POEPGES, 7

POEPLO, 5

POEVGES, 7

POHLMANN, 12

POLSTER, 5

PORTH, 7

POTSCHER, 4

PRASSE, 7

PRELLER, 4

PRIESHOFF, 12

PRIOHR, 8

PUESCHKE, 7

PUETZ, 7

PUNDT, 8

RAAB, 8

RAABE, 10

RABE, 13

RAECKER, 8

RAHMEL, 7

RAHTERS, 8

RALL, 3

RAMMERT, 7

RAMPENDAHL, 7

RAPS, 8

RASCH, 1

RASSMANN, 6

RATH, 14

RATHJEN, 3

RAUCH, 13

RAUDNITZ, 14

REBHAHN, 4

RECKUM, 4

REEDE, 1

REGENTHAL, 3

REHBEIN, 1, 3

RELMELMANN, 10

REICH, 3, 5

REICHARD, 4

REICHHARDT, 11

REICHHERZER, 1

REINEBACH, 1

REINECKE, 12

REINFELDER, 3

REIS, 4

REISING, 3

REISLAND, 7

REISSENWEBER, 4

REMSHARDT, 11

REMY, 14

RENNER, 4

RESE, 7

RESING, 3

REST, 10

REU, 5

REULEIN, 4

REUTER, 4

RHODE, 10

RICHARD, 13

RICHTER, 5

RICKER, 8

RICKERTS, 1

RIDDER, 8

RIECKE, 7

RIEDER, 4

RIEHN, 11

RIEKE, 1

RIEKMERS, 2

RIEPE, 10

RIEPERMANN, 13

RIES, 3, 14

RIESSKAMP, 13

RIETMEYER, 10

RIGGE, 8

RINOW, 6

RITHMUELLER, 5

RITTER, 10

ROBERTS, 10

RODENBUSCH, 9

RODENSTEIN, 14

ROEH, 3

ROEHLKEN, 3

ROEHR, 7

ROEMIGHE, 13

ROHLFING, 8

ROHLING, 13

ROLDENBURG, 10

ROLF, 10

ROMMEL, 6

ROMMINGER, 4

ROPP, 1

ROSCHE, 1

ROSE, 7

ROSENBAUER, 6

ROSENBERG, 5

ROSENBUSCH, 4

ROSENFELD, 5

ROSENKRANZ, 1

ROSENTHAL, 4

ROTH, 10

ROTHERMICH, 10

ROTHERMUND, 12

ROTHERT, 1

ROTTENFELD, 3

ROTTINGHAUS, 13

ROTTNER, 6

RUDDE, 13

RUDELT, 13

RUDLOFF, 10

RUECHEL, 1

RUEGELIN, 5

RUEHLING, 2

RUETGERS, 7

RUETHER, 8

RUETZEL, 8

RUGBACH, 10

RUMP, 1

RUSSEL, 1

SAARHAYE, 1

SAAYENGA, 6

SAFFER, 3

SANDER, 6

SANDERS, 8

SANTER, 9

SARBERG, 1

SAUER, 10

SCHAEFER, 5, 6, 8, 9, 13

SCHAFFNER, 1

SCHARRER, 5

SCHATTING, 6

SCHAUMBURG, 5

SCHEIDEMANN, 1

SCHENK, 11

SCHIERENBERG, 8

SCHILDKAMP, 13

SCHILLING, 7

SCHILLMUELLER, 8

SCHLEGEMILCH, 3

SCHLIEPER, 10

SCHLINGER, 12

SCHLOSSER, 5

SCHLUETER, 10, 12

SCHLUMP, 7

SCHMAEDES, 8

SCHMEDES, 4

SCHMELZER, 5

SCHMIDT, 1, 3, 4, 5, 6, 8,
9, 10, 11, 12

SCHMITZ, 1, 2, 7

SCHMUCK, 12

SCHNEDLER, 12

SCHNEER, 5

SCHNEIDER, 1, 7, 9

SCHOBER, 5

SCHOLL, 6

SCHOLLER, 7

SCHONNEBECK, 7

SCHOPPE, 1, 3

SCHORFHEIDE, 7

SCHORR, 3

SCHRADER, 8, 10

SCHREIBER, 4

SCHREPPEL, 6

SCHRIEVER, 3

LaVergne, TN USA
12 October 2009
160445LV00008B/1/P